WHY?

Practical Lessons to Build a Life
That Matters

Griselle Paz

LifeLight Press, Inc.
Miami, FL

All rights reserved. No part of this book may be reproduced, stored in a retrieval system, or transmitted in any form or by any means – electronic, mechanical, photocopy, recording, or otherwise now known or created in the future, without the express prior written permission of the publisher, except by reviewers wishing to quote brief passages.

Although every precaution has been taken in the preparation of this book, the publisher and author assume no responsibility for errors or omissions.

Unless otherwise indicated, all Scripture quotations are taken from the New Life Version, Copyright © 1969 and 2003. Used by permission of Barbour Publishing, Inc., Uhrichsville, Ohio 44683. All rights reserved.

Scripture quotations taken from The Holy Bible, New International Version® NIV® Copyright © 1973, 1978, 1984, 2011 by Biblica, Inc. Used with permission. All rights reserved worldwide.

Scripture quotations taken from the Amplified® Bible (AMP), Copyright © 2015 by The Lockman Foundation. Used by permission. www.lockman.org

Scripture quotations are taken from The Living Bible copyright © 1971. Used by permission of Tyndale House Publishers, Carol Stream, Illinois 60188

Scripture taken from THE MESSAGE. Copyright © 1993, 1994, 1995, 1996, 2000, 2001, 2002. Used by permission of NavPress Publishing Group.

Dr. Myles Munroe, *Understanding the Purpose and Power of Men* (New Kensington, PA: Whitaker House, 2001), 34. Used with permission. All rights reserved.

Chip Ingram, *Love, Sex, and Lasting Relationships* (Grand Rapids, MI: Baker Publishing Group, 2003). Used with permission. Fair use. All rights reserved.

Copyright © 2025 Griselle Paz
Published by LifeLight Press, Inc.
www.LifeLightPress.com
ISBN: (paperback) 979-8-9912698-0-3
LCCN: 2024946135 (print)

Cover Design: Enrique "Sero" Cruz
Interior Design: Don Consolver
Back Cover Design: Alexa Paz
Author Photo: JG Photography

We hope you enjoy this book from LifeLight Press, Inc. Our goal is to provide high-quality, thought-provoking books that spark imagination, and uplift spirits. By nurturing a community of artists, poets, dancers, writer and thought leaders, we aim to amplify voices that uplift, empower, and guide individuals on their journey of self-discovery and fulfillment.

LifeLight Press, Inc.
Miami, FL

Printed in the United States of America

Dedication

To Cristian,

who loves truth and strives for living a life of meaning

To seekers,

To those on life's journey searching for answers

How to Read This Book

Think of this book as a toolbox for your life. You can move through it from start to finish, or you can flip straight to the topic you need right now—whether that's purpose, manhood, work, money, God, or something else on your mind. However you choose to read it, here's how each chapter is set up so you can get the most out of it.

1. Every Chapter Starts with a Real-Life Question

We begin each topic with an important question many of us ask at one point or another. It sets the stage for what we're about to unpack and gives you something meaningful to reflect on.

2. Your WIFM (What's in It for Me?)

Right away, you'll see why this chapter matters. This quick section shows you exactly what you can expect to gain—clarity, confidence, direction, or just a helpful nudge.

3. Why Am I Telling You This?

This brief section is based on learned life lessons. Here I share an important principle.

4. A Backstory to Bring It Home

Each chapter includes a bit of backstory—personal, honest, and practical. It helps connect the idea to real life so the lessons feel relatable, not theoretical.

5. Life Builders & Life Killers

Every chapter gives you two simple digestible sections:

- Life Builders: the habits and choices that make you stronger, wiser, and more grounded.

- Life Killers: the patterns that quietly sabotage your progress if you're not paying attention.

These are quick to read and easy to apply.

6. Mom's Advice

At the end of each chapter, you'll find a piece of "mom wisdom"—the stuff a mom might share with her kids. Advice from the heart.

7. One Key Point to Remember

Each chapter leaves you with one clear takeaway. Think of it as the main idea you can carry with you for the rest of the day.

8. A Guiding Principle from Scripture

You'll also find a short, scripture-based principle to help keep you focused.

9. Helpful Resources

If you want to dig deeper, each chapter wraps up with recommended books, videos, podcasts, or tools that can support your growth.

Read It Your Way

Start at the beginning or jump to whatever topic speaks to you right now. There's no wrong way to use this book. The goal is simple: help you take your next step with confidence.

Acknowledgement

My heartfelt thanks to Paula Joy Snyder of Snyder Press. Thank you, sweet friend, for your encouragement your guidance and your passion for bringing books to life. This book wouldn't have come to fruition without you.

Table of Contents

Preface ix
Chapter One: Purpose – Why am I here? 1
Chapter Two: Identity – Who Am I? 27
Chapter Three: Manhood – What does it mean to be a man? 49
Chapter Four: Love – What is love? 67
Chapter Five: Fatherhood – How can I be a
good husband and father? 91
Chapter Six: Marriage – How do I know she is Mrs. Right? .. 109
Chapter Seven: Work – What kind of work should I do? 137
Chapter Eight: Money – How do I manage my money? 155
Chapter Nine: Time – How do I spend my time? 183
Chapter Ten: God – Why God? 195

Appendices

A. The Father's Love Letter 219
B. God's Prayer for you 223
C. Get to know God 225
D. How to pray when you don't know how 227
E. How to find a safe church 229
About the Author 233

Preface

Have you ever wondered why you are here? Have you blamed your parents for bringing you into this world? Have you ever wished you weren't here? I know I have. It is a tough place to be. Sometimes we have so many questions and it seems like so little answers. I understand that torment and my hope is that with this book, your life journey might be made a little easier. I know that's a lot to aspire to, but I hope it becomes at least one light on your path.

I started writing this book for my son. It became even more important for me to finish it after a near fatal car accident that almost took my life. I thought that if I weren't around anymore, there were a few things I wanted to let him know. As I started writing I realized that maybe what I talked about could benefit others, especially those who are trying to figure things out. Why do I write? Because, I want people to experience hope and the

Why?

fullness of life. Because living a hopeless life is gut-wrenching and I don't wish it on anyone.

What you will get from me is straight talk, no fluff. A mix of the practical and the spiritual. *Is that even a thing?* Hey, I'll give it a shot here. You'll get what I call "life builders" and "life killers." And also, some advice and recommendations. This is my unique view of the world. I know it won't fit everyone. I also know that not everyone will be ready for some of the things I share. Despite it all, I write.

I share some stories about my journey and what helped me get through the many ups and downs of life. I learned that in life it is not "win or lose," it is really "win or learn." What I am saying is that it's important to learn the life lessons and to use them to find your courage for living.

As humans, we may carry a hole in our heart. When we can't bear it, we try to fill that hole. Some of us try to fill it by being the center of attention or the clown. Others become workaholics. Some go to extreme sports. No matter what it is, at the end of the road, we usually come up empty. So now what?

Preface

In my specific case, when I got to the end of my road; it was turning to the spiritual that helped me get through. I get it, it's hard believing in God these days. It's hard to believe in anything.

This book is my humble attempt to offer thoughtful reflections on some of life's enduring questions. Who died and made me an expert? Well, let me tell you a quick story.

I used to live in a five-floor walkup apartment in Astoria, Queens. It was a cramped two-bedroom apartment that lacked closet space and could have easily been a dump but Mom made it a home.

From the kitchen window you could see the church steeple of Most Precious Blood Catholic Church. And you could hear the church bell that rang at the top of the hour.

My mother kept an open Bible on the top of her dresser in her room. It was really more of a decorative item since I never saw anyone read it nor was encouraged to read it myself.

I frequently heard God stories when my aunts and uncles would visit but it all seemed pretty empty to me. It always seemed like they had sad stories to tell while they begged God for whatever

Why?

they were believing for. There was no power in any of it.

Our Sunday mass was ritualistic, the mood was always somber and statues always showed Jesus, bleeding and suffering. Honestly it was rather depressing.

One day while at church, I asked God, *Seriously, is this all there is to you, sit, kneel, stand? Battles have been fought in your name, painters have painted you throughout the ages and all we get is sit, kneel, stand? There's got to be more to you than some empty ritual. God, show me the light.*

Little did I know that God was actually listening. This was a starting point for me. When I spoke those words, I actually activated a promise that God made.

> "If any of you lacks wisdom, you should ask God,
> who gives generously to all without finding fault,
> and it will be given to you." (James 1:5 NIV)

Why would God have listened to me? Who was I anyway to ask God for anything? But what I later came to know is that God is always there for anyone who is really trying to find Him.

I was working in New York and I moved around to various cities pursuing my broadcast writing career. I ended up in Atlanta at CNN. At that time in my life, I was trying to find God. I went to about 13 churches and nothing seemed right. I was ready to quit because I was just exhausted with coming up empty. So many of those churches seemed so lifeless. I was sharing my frustration with a young man that I knew and he said "why don't you try my church?" I said, "No, I really don't want to go to one of those mega churches." He simply replied: "You tried a bunch of them you might as well try one more." I thought, *why not, what can it hurt?* When I walked in, it was different. The church was packed.

There was a massive choir and when they started to sing, they raised the roof. It was like nothing I had ever experienced before. There was actually life in that church. It was a bible-based church. Everything the pastor preached came directly out of that book. For the first time in my life, I heard about the God not as just a bunch of words but as a living God that loves people and has good things in store for everyone. It just blew my mind. The very last church I went to was the one where I found God.

What I discovered from that experience is that when your heart

Why?

aches, when you are alone, when no one can help you and you look for God, He always shows up. How utterly remarkable!

It is tough being a believer these days. People immediately think that you are an uptight, critical, homophobic hypocrite. I get it. Why wouldn't someone jump to that conclusion, particularly when that's all they have ever experienced from so called "Christians." The word of God says, "we are therefore Christ's ambassadors, as though God were making his appeal through us." (2 Cor. 5:20 NIV) Yikes! I can honestly say we are not doing a great job of it. The delivery system has been lousy except for a few exceptions.

What bothers me the most is that in the meantime there are people hurting. I realized through my experience that just like me, there are many other people out there looking for answers. But because they have been treated so poorly in churches, they don't want to have anything to do with God.

The point is that I am tired of seeing people hurting. We dull the pain in so many ways, with drugs, alcohol, self-harm, sex, you name it. We even try God and retreat. I'm not trying to sound like a commercial for the Almighty One. I know that everyone isn't going to be into God. I am just saying this is my story, this is what I learned and maybe it can help you.

So yes, I am not an expert, a guru, a whatever, I am just another human being like you trying to make sense of things. Even if we don't see eye to eye, I hope that what I share will be useful.

If even a single insight brings you comfort or lightens your burden, then every step of my journey will have been more than worthwhile—and my life will have mattered.

Embrace the journey, for it is truly worth taking.

CHAPTER ONE

Purpose

Question: Why am I here?

What is in it for me?

A revolution. A life where you are energized and fulfilled. Knowing that what you bring to this world is unique, memorable, and impactful.

Why am I telling you this?

Pure love. I am passionate about seeing you live the happiest and best life you can live. Knowing your purpose is powerful. Purpose is your fuel for life. It is what makes you get up in the morning with radical energy and makes every day worth living. Purpose is what gives back to you a hundred times over when you see the reality of that purpose showing up in your life. Even better than that, is when you see your purpose changing others around you for the better. When your light ignites a fire

Why?

in someone else, there is nothing like it. It's an amazing gift that will supercharge your life.

The Back Story

Have you ever gotten the feeling that you don't quite fit anywhere in this world? I always felt like I was a little bit different. I really wasn't a "joiner" or a "follower." I didn't want to do things just because they were the "thing" to do. If it was the "in" thing to do, I usually went in another direction. I didn't want to be like everyone else. I wanted to be different. I wanted to be unique. I found most things boring, and I wanted to live an exciting life. I wanted to do things differently than my parents. I wanted a different life for myself. I remember at one point being really angry at my parents because I felt like I never asked to be brought into this world. What the heck was the point anyway? At school, kids and even some of the teachers would pick on me. I remember one who told me that I was dumb and would never do anything with my life. You know, because Puerto Rican girls from the Bronx are only good for getting pregnant and living on welfare. I got tired of being told I was either nothing or I was invisible. I got tired of being treated like a cliché.

Chapter 1 – Purpose

I remember being so angry that I made up my mind to show everybody just how wrong they were about me; I was neither a tramp nor a dummy. And I certainly wasn't going be a statistic.

Of course, now I had to deal with another set of problems. I put up with a lot of junk from other kids because they said I was the "brain" and the "teacher's pet" and "the good girl." I went from being invisible to being predictable and boring. You just can't ever satisfy people. No matter what I did, somebody had an opinion and a label for me. You know what, "whatever." I made up my mind that I was going to be somebody.

I studied really hard. I had to. I wasn't one of those kids that could see information once and just remember it. I had to repeat the info over and over, but I hung in there. I got good grades in high school and made it into college. Many people told me that education was the way to go, that it would change my life and in a way it did.

I graduated from college and took a job at a convention hotel in New York. At the time I thought I would work managing hotels in exotic locations. After all, now that I was an educated woman all the doors would open up for me, right? At least that's what I

Why?

was told. I worked in an exclusive part of the hotel taking care of the VIP guests who came in. One day the general manager comes in and says to me that I have to put on a baseball outfit because the World Series was being played in New York. If I was in the lobby, I wouldn't have minded; everyone else would have been doing it and there was a theme going. But how ridiculous was it to greet international guests who had no clue about the World Series in a baseball outfit in a part of the hotel that was supposed to be for the elite. Since I always spoke my mind, I said, "I suppose that when the shoe convention is in town, you'll want me to dress like a shoe." (There is such a thing by the way.) The general manager did not appreciate my comment. He said that I had to do it or I would lose my job. No one had told me that a college educated woman would have to dress up or be fired. So much for the world rolling out the red carpet because I got a degree. It sounds ridiculous now, of course, but at the time a picture was painted for me that my education would be my ticket to freedom. I decided right there to go back to school and get a master's degree in Journalism. Work was just crazy to me. Studying is something I knew how to do. So, I decided more education would be the answer.

Chapter 1 – Purpose

I did my master's and, although it was hard, I loved it. I was excited about my journalism degree. I had a wonderful professor who believed in me and helped me out. He knew some people at ABC New York and I got my first professional job in journalism as a desk assistant for ABC Radio. Most everyone was really nice. There was this one guy who was a pain in the neck with his condescending attitude toward me. I just brushed it off and repeatedly told him that under all that arrogance he truly liked me. Eventually I think he even became convinced of it himself. You can't put someone down who won't allow it to happen.

My career in Journalism began and my purpose became clear to me: to tell people the "truth" so people can make good decisions for their lives. Doesn't that sound wonderfully noble? It was noble in fact, but it is not the way the world works.

After ABC Radio I went to work for ABC News One. This is the department that sends news feeds to all the affiliate stations around the country. I enjoyed the work very much. It was really satisfying. There I was in my twenties in New York working as a writer. I had a dream job. I was a hit at parties. Everyone wanted to meet the writer from ABC New York. It didn't take long for

Why?

me to figure out that the reason they wanted to know me had more to do with what they thought I could do for them versus really getting to know me. But that didn't matter-I finally felt important. I did it. I finally felt like somebody. I proved that I wasn't stupid or a statistic.

I felt good about myself because of my job. I went on to work with other important companies like Univision and CNN. As I continued in my career, I started asking questions. Let me see if I understand this clearly: I have a master's degree; I have been nominated for an Emmy; I speak 5 languages; I have been in this business for almost a decade yet I am working as a contractor, on a night shift, making 40K/yr. with Wednesdays & Thursdays off and no chance for promotion. I might be able to get my own TV show if I have sex with the VP of news like my colleague did. So, despite being educated, I would still have to sleep my way to the top – did I get that right?

I got other offers like that. Be my lover, he said, and I will give you an editorial position at a top international magazine. I was told by the current girl he was having sex with that I would be a fool not to take the opportunity. After all, she had and was now

Chapter 1 – Purpose

the editor of a top fashion magazine in Paris. I could have had the Valentino dresses and an apartment in Milan. The problem was that I wasn't for sale.

I had position, access to celebrities, went to great parties and events in NYC, but at the end of the day I had to compromise my values to get anywhere. It was a slap in the face. Was I willing to say to myself that the six years I had spent in college were a joke? That everything I worked for meant nothing. I wasn't being lofty and self-righteous. I just wanted to believe that I had more value than what everyone else told me. I started to doubt my worth, so I found ways to convince myself that I was important. I thought I was important because I was educated. Then I thought I was important because I was a writer. Then I thought I was important because I became a wife and mother. It didn't occur to me that I was important just because I exist.

The fact that I am alive validates that I am worthwhile. I went in a lot of directions, thinking they were the right path. I thought that different things would lead me to living a satisfying life, but nothing made me feel better on the inside. Nothing I did got me closer to my purpose.

Why?

Why am I here? What is my purpose? Could it be that I'm meant to seek truth—because in truth, there is freedom? Maybe that was why I chose journalism. This was youthful idealism. I had not considered the messy negotiations with editors, the pressures, the limits of objectivity, and the ways truth itself can be subjective.

> *The Truth will lead you to freedom*

For me truth and purpose came when I developed a deep and intimate relationship with my Creator. When I was young, my parents and I used to attend a Catholic church. For me that experience was a rigid ritualistic thing devoid of power. I thought, *is this superficial stuff all there is to God?* I needed to understand who God was and who I was in relation to Him. I needed to understand why I was here. As I began to understand how God sees me, I started to see that I was important and valuable. My worth was not determined by others or by what I did. My worth was determined by the fact that God loves me. I realized I couldn't connect to my ultimate purpose until I connected to the ultimate source of truth and freedom. That discovery completely changed my life.

Chapter 1 – Purpose

How do I start to find my purpose?

Start by asking good questions. Good questions, did you get that? Questions that your brain can answer. Not self-defeating questions. Not "Why does this always happen to me?" But rather "What can I learn from this that will change my outcome?" See the difference? Good questions can make a huge difference.

No matter where you find yourself, here are some things to consider in figuring out your purpose.

1. Figure out your assignment. What is that one thing that you keep coming back to? What comes up over and over again? What do you want to fix in this world? If it upsets you, you probably have passion for it. If you see the problem, you are probably the right person to do something about it. If you see it, you own it.

2. Do something you like, not something you hate. Do you feel good about it? What do you feel excitement, or intensity about? Figure out what is producing good results. If you are not getting results in a minimum of three years-a maximum of four maybe that's not what you should be doing. I understand sometimes things take a long time before they materialize. My point here is "if the horse is dead, dismount." Don't try to make a square peg fit into a round hole.

Why?

3. Do what comes naturally. What flows out of you? Is it a desire to create, to build, to manage, to educate, to speak, to sing, to fly, to counsel, to organize, to heal, to communicate?

4. Be unique. Try something new. Explore your interests. You will find your gifts and talents as you try different things. Try something no one else has. People who are wildly successful have made it because they leveraged their uniqueness. Your value is in being you.

5. Take small steps to your destiny. Start by doing something. By taking action you will discover if you are headed in the right direction.

6. Get a mentor. What do mentors see in you? Can a mentor give you some insight into the talents he or she sees in you? Can this person, give you some pointers that could help you to get to where you are going? Be open to hearing suggestions. After you consider what the other person has to say. Does it resonate with you.? If it does, you'll know you are on the right path. Anyone can give you an opinion, but it has to feel right to you. By the way, if you look around and you don't see anyone that can mentor you remember that in today's world, we can access anything on line. There are videos, podcasts, books, seminars, conferences etc. This can be a good place to start.

7. Stay on track during the journey. Will you stay accountable when you are in a zero-visibility job in the middle of nowhere?

Chapter 1 – Purpose

Will you show up on time? This is a period of preparation. No one gets to his or her destiny without preparation.

8. Be dependable in your function. Each player is important to the end result. In a Super Bowl is any one player more important than the collective team? Own the vision, not the position. Serve the common goal with humility.

9. Serve others. Your gifts are given to you for the benefit of others. You are accountable for the gifts you have been given. Your gifts show the Creator's love for humanity. True leadership is serving others.

10. Love people. Your destiny includes people. Be the kind of person that sees the best in others, forgives the worst, and always hope. Don't let disappointments short circuit your destiny.

11. Occupy your destiny. Destiny is not just a place where you arrive. It's a place where you put down your stake and claim it as your own.

12. Trust God. He is the one that opens the doors and promotes you. Don't allow fear to derail you. If God told you that something is yours, believe it. Do not let anyone convince you that you don't have a purpose. You aren't here just to take up space: to pay bills and taxes, to suffer through and die. Why would you be here for that? You have special gifts and talents. Your creator will make clear what these gifts are and will give you the natural ability to perform them.

Why?

13. Believe in yourself. Believe that you have what it takes. Don't let doubt crush you.

14. Get a team. If your co-collaborators already support you and do the work for free, they will certainly do it for pay.

15. Trust God's protection. If you are not there yet, you may still be in training. God will never take you somewhere prematurely. Wherever He takes you, He will sustain you.

16. Be the leader who you would follow.

A few words on gifts and talents

You have specific gifts and talents that make you unique. They are gifts that are not only unique but vital to enriching the lives of the people around you. These gifts are light for those who may be looking around trying to find their way. What you think may be a small or insignificant thing could be the very thing that will inspire someone else. The people who cross your path will gain by what you have. It will either make them aspire to greater things or it will grate on their nerves so much that it will help refine their personalities. Understand that you are a vital part of life's ecosystem. No one else can give to the world what you have. Use your talents. It is selfish to keep from others. Don't hide that special part of you that only you can contribute.

It is like having a puzzle: without the part you play, the picture is not complete.

You may not figure things out right away but don't stress, relax. The answers eventually come. Be gentle with yourself. Don't get frustrated. Be patient. Consider the following tips for success.

Life Builders:

Confidence

Confidence empowers you. It is not arrogance. Confidence is a calm assurance that things will work out in your favor. You could say it's positive thinking. Confidence opens doors and leads to success. A man who is sure of himself rallies people behind him. Confidence is the sexiest quality a man can have and people sense it. People want to follow your light. Use your confidence to impact others' lives.

By now you are probably thinking, "well isn't that's great. Rah, rah, rah, thanks for being the cheerleader. But, what good does it do me to hear how great it is if I don't feel that way on the inside?" Being aware of a problem is always the first step to changing things. I'll say it again ask yourself some quality questions.

Why?

1. What do I believe about myself?
2. Did somebody put me down? Do I believe what they said?
3. Is my thinking holding me back?
4. Where am I getting my ideas about my self-worth?
5. Is my self-worth tied to a specific job, person or limiting belief?
6. Do I only feel good about myself when I have money?
7. Am I afraid of something?
8. Is it time to just jump in?
9. What can I do to change my situation?

Getting your self-worth from people or from money will ultimately let you down. Don't rely on either one. Change your focus and you can change your world.

Personal Power

You are more powerful than you probably give yourself credit for. Personal power is when you take action and produce meaningful results no matter what may come. There will be people and situations that may discourage you. Remember, you cannot relinquish your personal power, not for anyone. You will be faced with situations that test your character, integrity, and patience. There will be times when you want to quit because there doesn't seem to be any reason to continue.

Chapter 1 – Purpose

No matter what never give up.

President's Day weekend 2009, my family and I went to the Kennedy Space Center and we met Astronaut Story Musgrave. At the "lunch with an astronaut" event, Story said two very important things in response to the question "What advice would you give to someone who struggles with motivation?" I am paraphrasing Story's reply, but the gist of it was that you have to always go forward and you can't let circumstances defeat you. He told the audience that his family had a history of multiple suicides. He said that instead of allowing those tragedies to destroy him, they were exactly the fuel that he needed to go forward. If he had allowed these tragedies to take over, he would have given up his personal power and would have been controlled by those already in a grave. You can't allow family history, curses, or stories, to determine your future. You can't allow others' criticism or cynicism to define who you are. Clearly families have a great influence to either give you wings or put the final nail in your coffin. Your decision is whether you will live in freedom or as the living dead.

There will be times when things in your life don't seem to make

Why?

sense. I have faced times when nothing was going right. I have lived through not having a clue as to my purpose or passion. I have been in situations where it seemed like there were no answers. Sometimes I had to live with the fact that there was nothing I could do to change a situation or the people involved in the crisis. What I learned was not to lose my focus. What I learned was not to let others poison my spirit. I had to concentrate on what was right versus what was wrong. Believe me, I did plenty of crying and bellyaching over things that were completely discouraging. It got me nowhere. It made me angry and bitter and I lost so much precious time ingesting the poison of discontent. Discontent stemming from betrayals, hypocrisy, hurtful relationships, selfishness, disappointments, etc. You need to work with the life you have because it's the only one you have. Circumstances can rob you of your future. I wasted a lot of years being angry and no one cared, no one ever accepted accountability for his or her part in my pain and suffering. I spent years waiting for people to own up to their piece of it and it never happened. I got cheap excuses at best. What I learned was that I gave people a lot more credit than they de-

> *Winners never quit, and quitters never win.*

Chapter 1 – Purpose

served and I spent way too much time licking my wounds and expecting justice. I was the one in charge of my own justice. I was the one who needed to let myself off the hook and just get busy with the task of living. I guess my sense of fair play got the better of me. Life is not fair at times. Not everyone plays by the rules. As long as you are living, you will be hurt. So now that you know, here is another bit of information: once you get comfortable with the fact that things won't always go the way you want, then you can excel. This is where you find freedom's door. When circumstances don't define you, when people can't hurt you, when you learn to take yourself lightly, when you stop panicking-then you can truly be free. What would that look like for you? Can you see the potential for being all that you can be when you get to that point? It doesn't come in a day. It may come with a lot of pain. Sometimes it comes with a lot of kicking and screaming, but it comes if you are open.

Some of us listen to advice and some of us just have to learn the hard way. I should have figured this stuff out a long time ago, but all of it eluded me. I was in a box and had no idea how to get out. I didn't have the strength or the hope to pull it off. I'm not going to kid you: as I read some of the things that I have

Why?

told you, I say to myself, "Practice what you preach!" Some days it's easier than others for me to do what I recommend. Time after time I fell to my knees, praying for a way out of the prison of disempowering beliefs. I had to regain my focus. I found it every time when I looked to God as my source of hope. What I now understand is that every time I allow people to take away my joy, I give them my personal power and they get the upper-hand because I am allowing them to manipulate me and influence my actions. Keeping your peace and your joy keeps you in control. What's the alternative? Do you allow everyone to yank your chain for the rest of your life while you are unhappy and miserable? That doesn't sound like a good alternative to me. Someone you know might be extremely gifted at getting on your last nerve. The unrelenting onslaught is enough to make you go stir crazy or end up in cardiac arrest. It is for dealing with people such as this that you need to be equipped. If their opinions or criticism don't add to your destiny ignore them. Never relinquish your personal power.

Chapter 1 – Purpose

Life Killers:

Excuses

Someone once told me that excuses are nothing more than a justification for failure. "It's so hard" and "I can't help it" are probably the most overused excuses of all.

> *Excuses are nothing more than a justification for failure.*

Could it be that they are just a way of not taking ownership of a problem? After all, if it's somebody else's fault it gets you off the hook. I believe that people who make excuses run the danger of falling into a pattern of living below their full potential. Excuses can lead people down the road of mediocrity. There comes a time when we all need to be honest with ourselves and define what a fulfilling life looks like for us as individuals. We can only control ourselves and our own personal choices not that of others. I know for myself, I had to ask if I was willing to take responsibility for my choices. I had to choose not to see myself as a victim. I know that it takes courage to live an extraordinary life. My questions to you are: Do you want to be unstoppable? Do you want to defeat the fear that is holding you back? I encourage you to face whatever it is you

Why?

are afraid of and overcome that challenge. If you are scared, "do it afraid." Jumping into the unknown is scary but also rewarding. Do you

> *Jumping into the unknown is scary but also rewarding.*

want to justify where you are or do you want to go for what you really want? Don't wait for "perfect" circumstances, there is no such thing. You will wait your whole life if you hold out for perfect. If you try to live with a safety net, you will never truly fly. How can you soar attached to a tether?

Mediocrity

Mediocrity is a plague. A mediocre person is a forgotten person. Why? Because a mediocre person does not make a mark of any kind. It's the equivalent of being invisible. Mediocrity does just enough to get by. A life of excellence with all its potential and challenges doesn't come by doing the minimum. Living in a box where you don't step out, where you don't dare to be bold, is just as good as being dead. If you ever find yourself in that place and don't know how to get out, just take one small step. Success is not made of one giant leap, but of a lot of little steps. Every day make up your mind to take one step toward doing things differently. If it's the difference between making a fresh

Chapter 1 – Purpose

pot of coffee and drinking the stale stuff from a day ago, go the extra mile and brew that fresh pot. If the boss asks you to have the papers on his desk by Wednesday, have them for him by Tuesday. Take baby steps. You might ask, why bother? What's in it for me? Why should I do that for my boss when he's a tyrant anyway? Because a good dose of healthy pride goes a long way. Healthy pride allows you to prove to him and to yourself that you don't let your circumstances define you. It proves to you that you are not your circumstances; that you rise above. Having an attitude of excellence attracts people to you and makes them want to rally behind you. When you are different people take notice. Mediocrity offers you an average life, an average job, average friends, an average existence. There is more to life than average. This doesn't mean that if your life consists of a certain routine that it is no good. Even Oprah has a daily routine, and she leads what most people would consider an exciting life. The reason is that people like her buy up opportunities and always treat life with a sense of wonder. It is the wonder that makes life great. Mediocrity always says, "I'll take this step but it's as far as I'll go" and you would be right; it is as far as you will go. Mediocrity is living in limits and being okay with limits.

Why?

Toxic Pride

Toxic pride is a stumbling block. This kind of pride says, "I know it all and I don't need you." How can someone know when they are being prideful? When people are argumentative, unteachable, unforgiving, full of themselves, then they are probably in toxic pride. Toxic pride convinces people that they can only rely on themselves. It closes people off to others. There is always something to learn from others. Don't cheat yourself by closing your ears to what someone has to say. That doesn't mean you listen to just anyone. Be mindful of the voices you allow to speak in to your life. As long as you choose wise counsel you will be okay.

Don't allow toxic pride to keep you from God's best for you. The greatest position of power is on your knees. If you are too proud to assume a posture of humility, you will effectively block your ability to get wisdom regarding the challenges you may be facing.

When you are in a situation where you see no way out, when you are in a situation where you don't know what to do, the only one that knows the perfect answer is your Creator. Toxic pride has various expressions: criticism, impatience, judgment, insecurity, hatred, and selfishness. Check yourself. When you see any of these expressions, you'll know that you are walking in pride. You are not doing yourself any favors. This is the quickest way to get into isolation and despair. You can avoid a lot of trouble by avoiding toxic pride.

Why?

Mom's Advice:	Trust God with your destiny.
Key Point:	You are a light in the world. You were born at this specific point in history to share your gifts and talents for the benefit of others. You are no accident. You are here to fulfill a purpose. You are the only one who can fulfill it and you are the only you there will ever be. You are the piece of the puzzle that completes the whole picture.
Guiding Principle:	"Then you will know the truth, and the truth will set you free." (John 8:32 NIV)
Recommended Resources:	On purpose: *The Purpose Driven Life*, by Rick Warren On purpose: *Where do I Fit?* by Gary Keesee (CD Series) On purpose: *Start with Why*, Simon Sinek On happiness: *The Great Eight*, by Scott Hamilton On successful living: *The Secret*, by Rhonda Byrne On victorious living: *Your Best Life Now*, by Joel Osteen On Purpose: *Simon Sinek Masterclass: The Key Steps to Finding Your Purpose*
	*https://www.youtube.com/watch?v=XZ5NaZ2Ucdo*

Chapter 1 – Purpose

Notes:

Chapter Two

Identity

Question: Who Am I?

What is in it for me? Happiness and a great life.

Why am I telling you this?
Having a healthy self-image is one of the keys to a happy life. You were born to be a leader because you are meant to have a life of significance; not just success.

The Back Story:
Bill was a life coach. Every year he would put together a personal development conference. He gave people advice on how to achieve their dreams. His enthusiasm was infectious. Bill rallied people behind him. He called people to action. Bill was charismatic. As a life coach he spoke about being focused and unstoppable. Bill talked about clear communication and saying what you mean. He gave advice on changing your

Why?

thoughts to change your destiny. Bill really inspired people to live their dreams. On the surface he was really polished, a great role model. He was the picture of a loving husband and father. Unfortunately, that was all show. In his personal life he did not live the values that he spoke about, such as honesty and integrity. After he got people to sign up for his very expensive programs, he did not give them the mentoring he had promised. He did not answer phone calls. He picked favorites. He worked with those who promoted him. He ignored those he felt were irrelevant. He had a strong support team and a loving wife who was a major contributing factor to his success. He was admired and received gratitude from a multitude of people. As he did, he got a big head. So much so that he ultimately cheated on his wife. In public, she was everything to him. They were the perfect couple. Behind closed doors it was a different story. The next conference he put on wasn't nearly as well organized or as well attended. He ended up moving out of the country, leaving his children behind. His credibility was severely damaged. He was a fake. Bill spoke about the fact that in life it's not win or lose but rather win or learn. I know the things he experienced during this period of his life taught him a very hard lesson. Bill

Chapter 2 – Identity

began to rebuild his life. He reconnected with his children. He started building his business from the ground up. Bill had to learn that success without integrity is not success at all. Life without deep relationships is superficial. Remember, success is not as important as significance.

One in 400 trillion

Did you know that for those of us who are actually born we have already defied the odds? I read that there is one chance in 400 trillion of being born.*

That fact alone tells you that you were already born a champion. You are a living miracle. So why do so many people walk around being down on themselves? There can be any number of reasons. The key is not to let your past define you. It is important to know where you came from, but that doesn't predict where you are going. Don't allow the opinions of others to have an inordinate influence over you. Knowing how amazing you really are will give you the confidence you need to succeed. If the whole "you are a miracle" thing still doesn't convince you that you are

* Binazir, Dr. Ali *Are you a Miracle?* retrieved June 2, 2024 from https://www.huffpost.com/entry/probability-beingborn_b_877853

Why?

amazing, then consider the following: You were created by the Master of the Universe. Listen, I am not trying to get on a soap box and give you a speech, but here is what I discovered. I spent a lot of my life feeling bad about myself for a variety of reasons. One day I cracked open that Bible that was placed in the corner of the house like a decoration. To my amazement I found that it said some great things about me. I found out that I was created in God's image. How can I be junk when I am a mirror-image of God? I started thinking about the power of seeing myself that way and my whole perspective changed. If that wasn't enough to encourage me, I also found out that I was loved, unique, and precious. Wow, what a concept! I had only heard negative things about myself for so long that the idea that I was worthwhile just blew my mind. This was the beginning of my journey towards feeling whole.

Wholeness

The most important thing that you can do for yourself is to be whole. Don't drag into your present a cast of characters from the past; that makes for a very crowded life. Get rid of the clutter in your life. Open up that can of worms. It might not be pretty to look at but you will certainly feel a whole lot better once they're out of the way. It is impossible to enjoy your life and live it to the fullest if you are dragging the dead weight of the past with you. Okay, I get it. This is easier said than done. It requires cleaning up your side of the street. Looking at the past can be painful, but dragging it with you for the rest of your life is even worse. Sometimes we have to go through the pain in order to come out stronger. If you deal with your past and put it in its proper place, you give yourself the chance to enjoy the present and live. Do whatever it takes. Read books, go to a therapist, do personal development, talk to a friend, pray. I know it might not be the first things you would think of doing. And it might sound like a lot of trouble but there may come a time when you just have to do it. Sometimes, if you're going to live an extraordinary life you have to take extraordinary measures.

Get rid of the fear

Fear in any area of your life will paralyze you. You cannot move forward as long as you are living in fear. Fear will keep you on the sidelines. Fear will cost you your life. You need to push yourself regularly and move past what is familiar. This is how life is won. One bold move at a time. By the way, it doesn't matter if the step is big or small as long as you take a step. Don't look at

Why?

how far you have to go, just take a step daily toward your goals. Fear will tell you all the things that can go wrong. In a way it's trying to protect you. When this happens, tell fear, "Thanks for sharing but I am choosing to take this step of courage today." You will be amazed at how your life will change.

> *Don't look at how far you have to go, just take a step daily toward your goals.*

If fear is gripping you so hard and you don't know how to get unstuck, I recommend Rhonda Britten's book *Fearless Living*. Rhonda's fearless living program was life-changing for me. Anyone can give you advice. And sometimes when you get the advice you may be thinking "Duh! Tell me something I don't know." What was truly life changing about Rhonda's program was that for the first time ever I found a step-by-step guide to getting free. Not just advice, not just theory but an actual way to break the chains and that is priceless.

Passion

Passion is your fuel for living. Enjoy and live your life to the fullest. Your passion is your gift to the world. Don't bury it. Don't deprive others of it. Live to the extreme, love to the extreme.

When you are giving of yourself you are being the light that you were meant to be in this world. I used to think that there was no way I could live out the passion in my life. I had this "religious" idea that I had to give up the things that I loved if I also wanted God in my life. I thought He would judge me because I didn't want to be locked up in a church 24/7.

I thought life with Him would be boring. I was so wrong. I discovered that He is the one who gives me more passion for the things I love to do. I didn't trust Him. I questioned. Each time He took me by the hand like a loving patient father and showed me things I needed to learn. He met me where I was. He didn't hate the fact that I was different in fact He loved it. He loves those of us who are different. He puts the fire in us and is trustworthy enough to lead us to our best selves and our best lives. Make up your mind to live with passion. Life just doesn't happen to you, it's a decision. It may sound sophomoric, yet there is truth in this phrase: "You are what you say you are." If you believe you have a life full of passion, power, and love, that is exactly what you will have. Why? Because you are claiming it. If you are still wondering how to get passion, my suggestion is to do something every day that lights your fire. You nourish

Why?

your body daily, don't you? Why not do the same for your soul? Do something daily that keeps you alive on the inside.

> *Your words become your actions.*
> *Your actions become your habits.*
> *Your habits become your character.*
> *Your character becomes your destiny.*

(Lao Tzu, Chinese philosopher regarded as the founder of Taoism, 6th century BC)

Gratitude

A grateful heart opens the door to the best life has to offer. It is the launching pad of your dreams and to your destiny. Gratitude keeps you focused on what is good right at this moment and allows you to celebrate the present. So many times, people are focused on "I'll be happy when <u>fill in the blank</u>" happens. If you are always living for tomorrow, you will miss living today. If you are only happy when your circumstances are right, then you will live a very frustrated life. But if you are grateful, if you choose to focus on what is good in your life, all the other annoyances won't seem so bad or at the very least they will be tolerable.

Emotions can be up or down but with gratitude it's like setting

Chapter 2 – Identity

the thermostat to the best temperature where you can work, dream, live and thrive. Gratitude is good for you physically, psychologically and socially. You will sleep better, have more energy. You will feel happier and more optimistic. Gratitude will make you more generous, forgiving, compassionate, and outgoing. It will make you feel less isolated. When you focus on the good it allows more of the good to come in.

Complaining short-circuits blessings. It doesn't mean that life is perfect. It doesn't mean that you don't have complaints, burdens or hassles. It just means that you choose what brings a better result. Think of your brain as a tool. You can use that tool to build yourself up or to tear yourself down. The choice is yours. You have the power to make that decision and it is a decision. That doesn't mean you are going to wake up in the morning and automatically feel grateful. Somedays you will have to fight for it and fight hard. Somedays you will have to trap that negative thought and fight for your life like a junkyard dog. You will have to intentionally and on purpose think of the positive things in your life. Why? Because by nature we are all prone to think about what is wrong versus what is right. You live

> *Complaining short circuits blessings.*

Why?

with you 24/7; if you torture yourself with negative thoughts, you will wear yourself out. As a result, you won't have the drive to bring in the good things you desire in your life.

If you want to be grateful take inventory of what is good in your life, you have made it this far, certainly that's something to celebrate. There will be times when you'll feel that there isn't much to be grateful for and I get that especially if you are going through a difficult time. Maybe you can be thankful that nothing else has gone wrong. Or perhaps, that you have been able to withstand the season you are in. Maybe it can be as simple as having a good hair day. Start with whatever you have. Are you healthy? Do you have a place to live, food to eat, talents, love, gifts, and friends? If you start to think about it your list is probably longer than what you realize. Recognize that all the good in your life is a gift. Gratitude will reduce your stress and increase your self-worth. Celebrate the best of yourself and the best of others. Start a gratitude journal. It doesn't have to be anything more than just writing down, "today I am grateful for_____." Then review it once a week or once a month. You will be amazed how many great things you will find both big and small when you raise your awareness. Gratitude is one of your mightiest weapons for a happy life.

Life Builders:

1. **Integrity**
Always be a man of your word.

"Let your yes be a yes and your no be a no." (Matthew 5:37 NLV)

Show up even when it is painful for you and when it costs you something. It may cause you pain, embarrassment, money, or sacrifice but, regardless, keep your word. Your word should be your bond. Be direct. Mean what you say. Don't take people down rabbit trails of double-talk. Do what you promise. Don't do something wrong just because everyone else is doing it. Don't compromise on the little things. It is so easy to convince yourself that the little things don't matter. If you let the little things slip then how can you expect to be trusted with the bigger things? Whatever you do, don't join the crowd: don't be a people pleaser. A person of integrity is open and honest. A person of integrity is the same in public as he is in private. Integrity is a big word that only a big man can fulfill. Be a shining light, the world recognizes someone of integrity because it is so rare these days.

Why?

2. **Listen and respect others**

Be team oriented. Think of others first and build them up. Make sure you are making a difference in their lives. As you build up others and help them achieve their dreams, they will help you build yours. Everyone needs to feel valued, especially those who help you to be successful. If there is no respect for one another, it is impossible to be effective. For this reason, it is important listen carefully to the needs of others; this helps the team to stay engaged and feel valued. This is how all your dreams come to life. Be a servant-leader.

3. **Focus**

> *Distractions are the roadmap to failure.*

Focus is a major key to success. Rarely will you succeed at anything without being focused. You must be decisive and deliberate. Focus applies to everything. It doesn't matter what you are after, whether it's being a great athlete, a great scientist, a great writer, a great dad, a great husband, a great man of God. It all requires focus. So how do you stay on track? Keep feeding your goal with the right messaging. Read books that motivate you toward success. Put pictures on your wall of people you admire for their achievements. Do something every day big, or small, to help you perfect your skills.

Keep your eyes fixed on your goal. Distractions are the roadmap to failure. Consistency is the key to breakthrough.

> *Consistency is the key to breakthrough*

Anytime you look away from what you are trying to accomplish the easier it is to become discouraged or disinterested. Discouragement will come. Be aware of it and move on despite it; do it afraid, do it hurt, do it discouraged, just do it. Most successful men will tell you that you have to be relentless in your pursuit. There are certain truths in life and one of them is that if you lose your focus, you will lose your way. Don't let circumstances distract you. Circumstances, I guarantee, are temporary in nature and can be overcome. When you take your eye off whatever it is you are pursuing, it's like misplacing the target. If you lose focus, how can you know which way to go? A man without a plan is a man planning to fail. A lot of men have dreams, but the ones who achieve their dreams are those that stick with it. Nothing ever moves as quickly as we'd like; that is why it is so important to stay in the game. Re-group and continue the journey you started. Never tell yourself it is too late, because it is never too late.

> *Never tell yourself it is too late, because it is never too late.*

Why?

The only time it's too late is if you've quit. Giving up happens a long time before quitting. Recognize the signs and turn it around. Failure sucks: don't give up on you.

4. Finish what you start

This is a straightforward idea. You would not believe the number of people who don't bring things to completion. We live in a world of loose ends. A person can start with a great idea, and work on it with fire and enthusiasm, but somewhere along the line he or she stops. As soon as the challenges begin people cave in. If it doesn't work one way, try again. Thomas Edison failed thousands of times at making the carbon-filament light bulb and yet he didn't feel like a failure. He said, "I have not failed. I've just found ten thousand ways that won't work." Don't run at the first sign of trouble.

> **"Many of life's failures are people who did not realize how close they were to success when they gave up."**
>
> **(Thomas Edison)**

> *Vision without execution is hallucination.*

Keep at it until you succeed, because "vision without execution is hallucination," and yes, I did quote Edison three times. This is key: In time, people will forget your failures once you have succeeded. In the end, it didn't matter that Edison had not made it work 10,000 times but that he figured out how to make the light bulb affordable, long-lasting, and mass-producible. That one success revolutionized the world.

5. **Be resilient. Be resourceful.**

There will always be challenges – expect them and develop a plan for when they crop up. If there are things that come your way that you couldn't have possibly expected, then be tenacious. You have to find alternatives. Look at the problem from various points of view. Somewhere in between is the answer to whatever challenge you are facing. The one thing you can't do is turn away. Look for the possibilities. Look for the opportunities. Don't let the problem at hand be so overwhelming that you can't see past it.

The main thing to remember here is that there is more than one way to accomplish something. Use your creativity. Tap in to your network of people. Find out what is available out there for someone who is willing to put in a little more effort. If you keep your eyes open, you can tap into a variety of resources that will allow you to be efficient.

Why?

6. **Keep your legacy alive**

Your legacy, no matter what that is, cannot survive if there is no one to continue with the vision. Find someone who shares your passion and your vision. Train your successor. Share your wealth of knowledge. Teach so that that your work will not have been in vain. Entrust someone with the future. Share with other people what you know and allow them to bring their gifts to enhance the vision.

7. **Be a person of excellence**

What are the characteristics that you admire the most in people? What would you say about someone who is kind, generous, disciplined, courageous, gentle, patient, loving, fun, strong, peaceful, gracious, regal, revolutionary, and powerful. Would you say that person is someone worth following? Do you know anyone with those kinds of qualities? Common sense will tell you that in order to be the best it is wise to have a good coach or a mentor. Whose voice are you listening to? How do you want those characteristics to show up in your own life? How do you want to present yourself in the world? How you present yourself in your personal appearance and in your character shows the world how you feel about yourself. Is your life a message of excellence? Who are the coaches you want in your life? What part of yourself do you want to share with others? What you give to the world is the very best reason to pursue excellence and the very best way to leave a part of yourself that lives on even after you are no longer here.

Life Killers:

Laziness

Don't be lazy. Laziness is the biggest enemy to your life. Laziness is a thief. It wastes your time, it steals your health, it kills your ambition, and it destroys your opportunities. Laziness can't help you keep a job. It doesn't even give you a clean place to live. Laziness accomplishes nothing good. For everything, there is a time and a season. Make sure you don't take relaxation to the extreme of laziness. I know life can be overwhelming at times. I know sometimes life makes you feel like it's more than you can bear, but that is not an excuse for idleness. Regardless of how difficult things get, "It's too hard" are words that should never come out of your mouth. They are the beginning of the end because they signal defeat. Don't get discouraged, just do your best.

Why?

Arrogance

Don't be deceived into arrogance. It can creep up on you. It is easy to fall into thinking "look at all I have done, I'm amazing." "Don't you think I'm great?" "Look at what I've accomplished." If you're boasting, stop to think how your words are affecting others. Carrying on will affect your relationships. Sometimes you can think, "I don't need anyone I can do this myself; I don't need them." No one can live in a vacuum. We all need each other. Everyone has something that he or she can contribute. Everyone has a strength that you might need to make your life whole. Don't go around thinking that you are better than everyone else, that is a trap that leads to isolation. No one wants to be around people who are full of themselves all the time.

We may take on an attitude that says, "That's the least that I deserve given everything that I have done." Anytime that your expectation is for someone to satisfy a need, expect to be disappointed. People won't always see what you've done. You also shouldn't need the adoration so much. What are you missing that would make you need that?

Arrogance has many faces, so at times it can be hard to tell when it is happening. Arrogance can also take on a face of false humility: "Oh, I was just trying to do the best I could." If you enjoy the attention a little too much maybe you are dealing in arrogance. So what? You might say it's nice to get recognition. Absolutely; it is great to get recognition, but if you think that you are above others you will be a very lonely person. Arrogance says I am deserving, bow down to me. An arrogant person doesn't think he or she has to contribute-to the project, cause, or relationship. Arrogance will convince you that you don't need anyone. If you don't give of yourself and you expect to always take and be served, people will tire of you.

Why?

Mom's Advice: Serve others and they in turn will serve you.

Key Point: Be someone worth following. Would you follow you?

Guiding Principle: "Love and truth form a good leader; sound leadership is founded on loving integrity" (Proverbs 20:28 MSG)

Recommended Resources:

On your identity in Christ: *Who am I?* by Mike Shreve

On your identity in Christ: *Sonship* by World Harvest Mission
(This was revolutionary for me)

On loving yourself: *You're a Badass* by Jen Sincero

On beating fear: *Fearless Living* by Rhonda Britten https://fearlessliving.org/

On leadership: *The Mentor Leader* by Tony Dungy

Chapter 2 – Identity

Notes:

Chapter Three

Manhood

Question: What does it mean to be a man?

What is in it for me?

Having a clear vision of what it means to be a man will help you to live successfully in all areas of your life.

Why am I telling you this?

I don't want you to struggle or be confused about what it means to be a man. Once you understand your worth as a person, it is also important to understand your worth as a man. Having this knowledge will make you strong and grounded so that you can deal with everything that comes your way.

The Back Story

John never felt like much of a man. He was raised by a father who was harsh. Every word out of his mouth was demoralizing. They didn't share anything in common. John's father liked the

Why?

outdoors. John was happier building model planes. He dreamt of building things. He wanted to go to college and become an engineer. His father thought all a man needed was muscle to make a living, not an education. Growing up John's father spent a lot of time drinking and womanizing. John would have to drag his father out of bars with his mother and he hated it. Oftentimes his dad would get angry and beat him. And with every beating the father crushed his son's dreams. Any little boy who has ever had to endure the pain of being rejected grows up to be a man full of pain. Even though his father was physically there, John was emotionally abandoned. John had to figure out life on his own. It is difficult to become a man without any direction or guidance. It is unfortunate that so many boys and young men are left to fend for themselves. The wounds cut deep and it can take a lifetime to heal. All the rejection seemed to weigh John down.

At 14, John got his first job and once he knew he could take care of himself, he left home and never looked back. He went to two years of college but when he got his high school sweetheart pregnant, he quit school and started to work to support his family. He became obsessed with making money. In his mind,

Chapter 3 – Manhood

if he could make lots of money and afford to live in the fancy neighborhoods then that would mean that he was worthwhile. This was tragic for John because when he didn't have money for whatever reasons he felt like a failure. John was running. He was chasing after things that made him feel like he had value. All that he did stemmed from his father's disapproval. A father who said that a man uses his brawn and not his brain. They might as well have been from different planets. John needed to make a choice. Every man faces this choice sooner or later. A man can choose to live in the pain of his past or look boldly into his present and enjoy the life he has today. Even when a man doesn't have an earthly father, he does have a heavenly father that can guide him. A man can choose to turn things around for himself, for his family and for his future. Men are continually deceived into believing that they are nothing and won't amount to anything; that is not what God had in mind when he made you a man. There comes a time to stop thinking like a boy and realize that the only person responsible for your life is you. When you take on the responsibility of owning your choices you start on your path to manhood.

Why?

What does it mean to be a man?

I thought about this for a long time. What does it mean to be a man? Honestly, I had no idea what to tell you. I'm a woman, what do I know about what it means to be a man? Many of the men I had seen in my young life were either drunks, cheaters, abandoned their children, or beat their wives. The only thing I ever saw them do was work-if they weren't the lazy type. Seeing this behavior made me think that maybe the man's only role was to provide. To be honest, I think some men still believe that is their only job too.

I decided to do a little research. I came across a great book by Dr. Myles Munroe called *Understanding the Purpose and Power of Men*. This was an eye opener. I understood that man was designed to be not only the provider and protector, but also the visionary, leader, and guide. I had never heard of that before. Not only had I not heard it before but it dawned on me that a lot of men had not heard it either. My eyes were opened to the true value of a man. It made me realize that if men really understood what they were designed to do, they could impact the world in positive and profound ways.

Chapter 3 – Manhood

Dr. Munroe explained that the roles of men have changed. Is a man the one who fills a traditional role of provider? Or is a man one who shares the responsibilities for home and children while both spouses pursue careers? Or is a man the one who has gotten completely away from male stereotypes and has decided to be the one to take care of the kids while the wife works? Roles have changed for men. The problem is that if a man defines who he is by the role he plays, what happens when the roles change? How does a man know who he really is when there are so many different expectations? This kind of mixed messages can be so discouraging and confusing. Dr. Munroe said, that men "need to think in terms of purpose rather than roles. The reason men are having problems today is that they have been basing their worth on the wrong thing all along. Roles have never been the true basis of a male's identity and purpose. Roles can be helpful or harmful but ultimately they merely reflect culture and tradition. What men really need to discover is their underlying purpose, which transcends culture and tradition." Men were made by God to live a life of purpose, not to play a role.

Munroe, Myles. "God's purpose for the male" *Understanding the Purpose and Power of Men*, 2003, p. 34

Why?

Albert Einstein once said that **"the value of a man should be seen in what he gives and not in what he is able to receive."***

Could it be that a man's purpose is to leave the world a better place by what he gives? And as a man what are the things that he can potentially give? A man can start by giving of himself.

Dr. Munroe says that a man's first priority is to be the foundation of his family. A man can also protect and provide. And finally, he can be a visionary, a leader and a guide. Let's take a look at these attributes.

Man as a provider and protector

God gave the man work because it exposes a man's potential. If you place no demands on your potential, how can you show what you are made of? How can you prepare for fulfilling the purpose that God has placed on your life? God gave the man work because it is related to his purpose. His purpose is to stay in the presence of God and learn to manage what God has given him to do. The word provide comes from the Latin word meaning "to see ahead," or, in other words, to have vision

---

* "Albert Einstein Quotes." Quotes.net. STANDS4 LLC, 2021. Web. 27 Feb. 2021. https://www.quotes.net/quote/39860

and to move ahead those who are under your care. In American culture, when a man decides to get married, it is customary, at least in the U.S. to give his wife his last name, the significance of this is that he is responsible for her. If you ask a woman to marry you, she will ask "Can you sustain me?" Here I'm not referring to just money. I'm talking about comfort, knowledge, intellectual stimulation, protection and security. Man as the provider means that he is up to the task of supplying all of these things to his family. As a man you have been given physical strength, logical thinking, a sense of territorial protectiveness, and a drive to excel. Because of these attributes, you are able to protect. God has made you physically and psychologically able to fulfill your responsibility. You have the courage that it takes to protect. It is in your DNA as a man to meet the challenges of being a man.

Man as the Foundation for the Family

A man's priority is to be the foundation for the family. Isn't it true that when there is a good father in a home that the whole family is stronger? If the man is weak, if he has cracks in his foundation, the rest of the family is weak. A man needs to invest his time in knowing who he is in Christ first. I remember reading

Why?

in Myles Munroe's book *Understanding the Purpose and Power of Men* that a man needs to know that he is loved by God, that he is valuable and is set apart for doing great things. Wow, really? Had I ever seen this in anyone I knew? Only one man came to mind: my uncle. And I was thankful for having seen at least that one example. I thought about why he was so different than all the rest. My conclusion was that he put God first in his life. Then came his wife, then his children; these were his priorities.

My uncle always treated his wife with respect. He sacrificed for his family no matter what it cost him. He was always present and available for his sons and he led by example. So why did everyone else around me seem so broken? I think it's because men have lost their way. When a man sees himself as small and insignificant he cannot be who he was meant to be. This is why it is so important to value yourself. You can't give to other what you do not have. Your first job is to be strong. To love yourself. To know that you are valuable. Once you have secured these things in yourself you are able to live out all the other aspects of being a man. If you judge yourself by the superficial standards of the world, you will always feel inadequate. If you judge yourself by how well you are fulfilling your purpose, then you will know that you are succeeding.

God is the source of a man's strength, wisdom, and hope. When you are equipped with these weapons you are able to thrive.

Okay, I can see you rolling your eyes at me. God, always this God thing. So, let's put that aside for a minute. Think about your own life. Think about your relationship with your own father. How much stronger are you with him than without him? What if he was the kind of man who taught you and led you? What do you think your life would be like? What if you were receiving guidance versus figuring it out on your own? Could the load be a little lighter? What would that look like for you? Are there other men in your life besides your father that you look up to? How have they influenced your life? Was it your grandfather who taught you how to laugh? Was it your uncle who taught you how to be focused? Was it a friend who taught you how to dream? If you have been fortunate enough to have a man help you shape your life you know exactly what it has meant to you. The point is that when you put yourself in a position to receive wisdom from others you become stronger.

Why?

Man, as visionary, leader and guide

You may not feel like a leader or a visionary, but it is exactly who you were created to be. It is crucial for you to know yourself. It is far more important to know who you are in God's eyes. As you communicate with your Creator you will be given revelation and wisdom on how to live your life. God created man first and gave him the responsibility for everything. God entrusted man with his purposes. Man was to be the one who would guide his family. God chose man's purpose and design man to be the leader and guide. If you see yourself from His point of view rather than yours, you will begin to understand your purpose more clearly. As you gain confidence in yourself and your purpose you can begin to be the foundation for your family. And as each and every man steps up to this challenge, then society as a whole becomes stronger. As long as the man is stripped of who he was meant to be, everyone suffers. Wives have no husbands to turn to and children have no fathers to be their guide. This is why it is so important for you to know these things so that you do not get lost.

Why tell you this? Because I want you to be a man of integrity.

Chapter 3 – Manhood

To be the man you were destined to be. Men who are present and stepping up can change the world one child, one family, one community at a time. There is

> *Men who are present and stepping up can change the world one child, one family, one community at a time.*

power in your manhood. This is something to celebrate. Don't let anyone take that away from you.

Okay, so this whole business about being a man seems overwhelming, doesn't it? Just reading these few pages makes your head want to explode, right? I get it. It is a lot to take in. But it is not beyond reach. You are fully equipped to do and to be everything you were meant to be.

One of my favorite poems is Rudyard Kipling's *"If"*. I know what you are probably thinking: "did you really just go there?" Hear me out, don't quit on me. I know it's some old poem you've never heard. But I wouldn't bring it up if it wasn't important. So why do I think it's important? Because it gives great advice. It also speaks truth and as I've said before there is always freedom in truth.

It says...

Why?

If

If you can keep your head when all about you
Are losing theirs and blaming it on you,
If you can trust yourself when all men doubt you,
But make allowance for their doubting too;
If you can wait and not be tired by waiting,
Or being lied about, don't deal in lies,
Or being hated, don't give way to hating,
And yet don't look too good, nor talk too wise:
If you can dream – and not make dreams your master;
If you can think – and not make thoughts your aim;
If you can meet with Triumph and Disaster
And treat those two imposters just the same;
If you can bear to hear the truth you've spoken
Twisted by knaves to make a trap for fools,
Or watch the things you gave your life to, broken,
And stoop and build 'em up with worn-out tools:
If you can make one heap of all your winnings
And risk it on one turn of pitch-and-toss,
And lose, and start again at your beginnings
And never breathe a word about your loss;
If you can force your heart and nerve and sinew
To serve your turn long after they are gone,
And so, hold on when there is nothing in you

Chapter 3 – Manhood

Except the Will which says to them: "Hold on!"
If you can talk with crowds and keep your virtue,
Or walk with Kings – nor lose the common touch,
If neither foes nor loving friends can hurt you,
If all men count with you, but none too much;
If you can fill the unforgiving minute
With sixty seconds' worth of distance run,
Yours is the Earth and everything that's in it,
And – which is more – you'll be a Man, my son!

Kipling talks about qualities that are timeless. He says what so many mothers hope for their sons. He says what so many brides wish for in their husbands. He says what so many fathers want to leave as a legacy for their sons. Kipling's poem seems to be a lofty goal for any man. It is something to strive for. As long as you are doing your part to be the very best you can be, that is all anyone can ask.

The reality is that you do have the temperance (the self-restraint) so as not to lose your head. You have the courage so as not to doubt yourself. You have the patience to wait when it seems that the wait might never be over. You have the strength to not deal in lies and hatred, the trap that leads to bitterness. You have the wisdom to have a sense of yourself without letting things get

Why?

out of balance. You have the perseverance to never quit. Don't ever let anyone convince you that you do not have what it takes to be this kind of man. You are well able.

Life Builders:

1. **Be true to yourself.**

2. **Accept** who you are. Only you can be you so do it with excellence.

3. **Stand** for what is right even if the whole world is doing what is wrong.

4. **Live** your own life, not the life everyone expects you to live.

Life Killers:

1. **Listening to the negative opinions of others.** Don't worry about what other people say. Be your own man.

2. **Losing your Focus.** Look up never look around you. You were meant to soar with the eagles, not cluck with the chickens.

3. **Derailment.** Don't let bad influences, circumstances, or petty things derail you.

4. **Hopelessness.** Hopelessness keeps you living below your potential. It is a disabling spirit. It will keep you satisfied with where you are. The thought of changing or doing

better or living a different life won't even enter your mind. Hopelessness allows you to accept every excuse: I can't do it because I'm poor; because I'm too small; because I have a handicap; because I never had a stable home; because my parents are divorced; because my dad never encouraged me; because my mother was crazy; because I was hurt. Do you get the picture? You can insert whatever excuse you want – the end result is being paralyzed. It is accepting a mediocre life that you were never meant to live.

5. Don't be a victim. Get rid of that victim mentality. Don't waste your life licking your wounds. A victim mentality makes only one person the victim…you. It gives you a shabby self-image. So many times, you are just churning over and over what someone said and that person doesn't even remember it. Someone says something in a fit of anger and then lets go of what was said once he or she cools down. A victim holds on to those words for years. Who's in a cage now? Who's in bondage? You think if that person was unkind to you and that person was supposed to be your family and/or your friend, what you can expect of anyone else? Sometimes the people closest to you are the ones who are the cruelest. In the Bible there is the story of Joseph and in his life, it was his family members that treated him the worst. But he refused to have a victim mentality. He made up his mind to rise to the top no matter what the circumstances. In the end, he also forgave. Unforgiveness is also a victim's trap. The only one getting hurt is you. Not only do you feel victimized by other people

Why?

but you've also learned to do it to yourself. You've done it by isolating yourself from others, by not opening yourself to trust anyone, by churning hatred and negative thoughts within you. Who's torturing who? Meanwhile, whoever hurt you doesn't even have a clue. And if that person does not have a clue, he or she is not ready to be accountable, because of their problems or immaturity. And there you sit bashing your head against the wall because this person who is either clueless or doesn't have it together is hurting you. What's up with that? Move on and be happy. Take responsibility. Look at the word responsibility: it is the ability to respond. You choose how you will respond. Eleanor Roosevelt said that "No one can make you feel inferior without your permission." Don't give anyone permission to make you feel worthless. If you are doing so, it's because your self-worth is rooted in what others think versus being rooted in what you think of yourself.

Chapter 3 – Manhood

Mom's Advice:	Be your own man.
Key Point:	Understand what it means to be a real man. There is strength in that.
Guiding Principle:	"Every young man that listens to me and obeys my instructions will be given wisdom and good sense." (Proverbs 2: 1-2 TLB)
Recommended Resources: 	On being a man: *The purpose and power of Men* by Dr. Myles Munroe On Being a man: *Understanding true manhood* by Dr. Myles Monroe https://www.youtube.com/watch?v=vm4OwvgeujY On being a man: *Wild at heart* by John Eldredge On being a man: *He-Motions* by Bishop T.D. Jakes

Why?

Notes:

Chapter Four

Love

Question: What is love?

What is in it for me? Love is the ultimate prize when you know how to give it and how to receive it.

Why am I telling you this?

I am telling you this because I want you to have a satisfying life full of love. More than anything I want you to know that you are loved. You are wanted. You are precious. You are valuable. The greatest need of every human being is to feel loved and accepted. Until you love and accept yourself it will be difficult to love and be at peace. When you love yourself, you are able to give and also to receive love.

The Back Story

I know what it's like to live in the hell of feeling unwanted and invisible. I spent a great many years living there. I ran from

Why?

the pain. I tried to outsmart that pain but it caught up with me regardless. It took me many years to come back to life.

My biological father wasn't a part of my life. He didn't fight to keep me in his life. He never made me a priority. I felt irrelevant. I felt rejected. This record kept playing in my head. "If you're not special to your own flesh and blood, how do you expect to be special to anyone else." I reasoned that if I became someone important like a broadcast news writer then my father would have to realize just how special I was, and he would finally want to be a part of my life because he would realize what he missed out on. He would finally love me. I kept on trying to fix what was wrong on the inside with stuff from the outside. The problem with this approach was that I needed to constantly have more and do more and achieve more and have more conquests in order to feel right and in the end I felt empty.

I was born in a very small town in Puerto Rico. My mother worked in the mayor's office. My grandfather was known by just about everyone in town. They say when you live in a small town you live in a large hell. I can tell you that in my case this was true.

Chapter 4 – Love

I was a rape child. My father had slipped something into my mother's drink and taken advantage of her. She became pregnant with me. I was the constant reminder of that rape. I was unwanted. My mother was of the mind that children were meant to be seen and not heard. Every time I brought up the past. Every time I asked about my father, I was told to be quiet. I was told not to be *impertinent*. Impertinent, what an overpowering word that is. In other words, I was disrespectful, rude, inappropriate, and irrelevant. I was told to go off and play and stop asking questions. I was muted from that moment forward. I was invisible.

When I was sixteen, I asked my grandmother about the circumstances surrounding my birth. She repeated the same horrific story. I figured that she would know. After all, that was her daughter and she would've been there at that time to know exactly what was going on.

Here's the strange thing. During the summers my mother would make me spend time with the man who raped her because she said he was my father. Every time he came near me, I wanted to throw up. I used to run into the bathroom and hide. How was I

Why?

supposed to love someone who had violated my mother in such a way? Things didn't add up but I still couldn't figure them out; after all, I was just a child. I spent a lifetime hiding, pretending to have a perfect life because I was ashamed. I'd rationalize that if I was the picture of success and perfection people would love me and accept me. I always thought that I had to do more in order to be loved.

It wasn't until I was around 30 years old that I finally got the truth. And I got the truth from the man who had been demonized for all those years. Isn't it ironic that the only person who ever gave me the truth was the one that I least expected it from?

My mom became involved with a young man. He had a way with words. He was a charmer. He had dark hair and blue eyes. I think that was the combination that won her over. This charmer did nothing more than lead my mother into a passionate relationship. There was no rape. I wasn't the rape child; I was the love child. What a difference that would have made in my outlook on life if only I had known. Why the rape story? Well after all, my mom was the daughter of an upstanding citizen who had started a school, who was well known in the

Chapter 4 – Love

community and she did work in the Mayor's office. She had to save face. So, her darling sister who thought she could control everything came up with the idea of concocting the rape story. I know she was thinking of her sister but no one thought about the damage that it could do to me. I guess I should have asked my grandfather instead of my grandmother. He wasn't buying that story. He kicked my mom out of the house and told her not to come back ever again. My mom's other sister who had her own house took us in. I remember it was a simple wooden house with a couple of rooms but that was our home for a while.

By the time I was out of kindergarten, we were out of Puerto Rico and living in New York with the sister who came up with the rape story. We lived in the projects in upper Manhattan near 100th & Amsterdam. The only good thing about that was that we lived in the 20th floor and that kept us away from the chaos in the streets below. However, there was more violence in the home than outside, so it didn't really matter much. I remember one day there was a lot of yelling going on. I went to see and saw my aunt being beaten by her husband. My mom was trying to stop him and he hit her. When I saw this, I stepped in and tried to get him to stop. "Don't hit my mommy" as if that did

Why?

any good. He pushed me so hard that I flew into a wall and hit my head. I was knocked down to the floor. I don't know what happened after that: all I know is that eventually he stopped but by then my aunt was being taken to the hospital by ambulance. My mom rode with her and I was left in the apartment with my older cousins. Four kids left by ourselves while my aunt got patched up. Before I was six all I knew was that men raped, abandoned, and beat women. Maybe, I didn't know it as clearly as I articulate it now, but somehow that was the message left behind. The sad thing was that I had no father to protect me.

I spent most of my young adult life attempting to overcome the wounds that I felt deep inside. I felt invisible. I felt insignificant. Wow, did that ever do a number on me. People who knew me would never say I was that way. I was known for flying high, pursuing my dreams, being adventurous, living to the fullest, being fun, crazy, and still being able to keep myself together. Guys would tell me often that I was too much for them. I was too smart for them. Somehow, they were intimidated by me. On the inside I thought, *why should I dial it down just because they can't handle it?* I thought *they should love me for me* but that was quite elusive.

Chapter 4 – Love

I had a great step dad. He has always been there for me and is an incredible blessing in my life. At the time though I only saw my glass as half empty. I only felt the loss and the rejection. I didn't realize how great a gift he was and how merciful God had been to me by putting him in my life.

I had to drag myself out of this pit. To be honest I tried a lot of different things but they just did not bring the healing I had hoped for. I tried to stuff it. Sweep it under a rug. I learned early on that if you didn't look at it you didn't have to deal with it. The problem with that is that it's still there. I tried to get away from it by having a good time, going out, trying all kinds of entertainment. Partying, drinking too much. I tried being the center of attention. I tried to get myself out of the pit by being successful. Working hard to get noticed and validated. No matter what I tried, I still felt empty. Eventually I got tired of the pain. It was like carrying a bunch of rocks on my back. I honestly didn't know what I was looking for but I knew I didn't want to hurt anymore. Did I even consider God? No. It wasn't even a thought. In a moment of solitude, I thought to myself, *I wonder if there is anything I can use in that book? People keep trying to shove it down my throat like it has all the answers. Could they be right?*

Why?

It happened slowly, like when you dip your toe in the pool. I can't really explain how it happened, but each time I read the word of God it was like putting a healing balm on a bad burn. My life began to change. The lover of my soul was the one who gave me a sense of self-worth I had never experienced before. Little by little I started to discover His love for me and how He sees me. When I began to see myself that way everything changed. I know that it seems like some fantasy but it is my hope that you, too, will make this thrilling discovery.

I know now the importance of having a father. An earthly father and a heavenly Father. Our heavenly Father fills in the gaps where our earthly fathers fail. But, regardless, being a man is one of the most important jobs on this planet. Never underestimate the importance of simply being there for your family. Ask any little girl or boy who didn't have a father what it would have meant. Ask any man sitting in a prison cell how having a father to follow would have changed his life.

What is real love?

No matter the relationship-romantic, friendly or with family – there's a tender unmistakable warmth that lets you know when love is truly selfless. It is the gentle devotion that gives without keeping score, the compassion that lingers even on hard days and the natural desire to lift someone's spirit simply because you care. This is the quiet, way real selfless love makes itself known. If you are ever in doubt use this as a guide.

> "Love, endures with patience and serenity, love is kind and thoughtful, and is not jealous or envious; love does not brag and is not proud or arrogant. It is not rude; it is not self-seeking; it is not provoked [nor overly sensitive and easily angered]; it does not take into account a wrong endured. It does not rejoice at injustice, but rejoices with the truth [when right and truth prevail]. Love bears all things [regardless of what comes], believes all things [looking for the best in each one], hopes all things [remaining steadfast during difficult times], and endures all things [without weakening]. Love never fails [it never fades nor ends]."
> (1 Corinthians 13:4-8 AMP)

Measure your relationships by this guide. Most importantly, pay attention to what people do, not what they say. What they do tells you more about their hearts than anything else.

> *Pay attention to what people do, not what they say*

> "Greater love has no one than this: to lay down one's life for one's friends." (John 15:13 NIV)

Why?

Real love is actually more about giving than getting. Love in its purest form is sacrificial. It is a love born of God, born of His Spirit. It is the kind of real selfless love that

> *If you go to love looking to see what you can gain versus what you can give, it is not really love.*

gives even when there is no reason to give. It is the kind of love that hopes, that always believes in the best. This kind of love separates the men from the boys, because simply put this love is not selfish. This kind of love allows for failures and mistakes and still endures. This kind of love is truly a precious gift, but this is only one side of love. Coupled with this sacrificial love there should also be passionate love. It is the kind of feeling that overtakes you and makes you desire physical closeness with that special person. Just a word of warning on this subject. Playing on feelings of love for sexual pleasure is selfish and immature. Don't be confused between passionate love and sexual lust. If you go to love looking to see what you can gain versus what you can give, it is not really love.

Lastly, there should always be the friendship kind of love. In friendship, you share your hopes, dreams, adventures, and fun. This is the place where you are accepted for who you are.

Chapter 4 – Love

You are not judged but given a listening ear and a shoulder to cry on. In friendships you give to one another. You show each other preference. You take turns paying the bill and don't free-load off each other. In friendship you show each other kindness and understanding. You need all three kinds of love: sacrificial, sexual and friendship for a successful relationship. And one more thing a good dose of healthy self-love is also very important. When your tank is full and you feel good about you then it is easier to give into a healthy relationship.

Life Builders:

Understand the Love – Power Connection

Love, is a short word full of complexity. The power of love is boundless. All of your aspirations hang on love. Love is what supports everything else in your life. A marriage certainly cannot hang on without love, and neither can a family. Your career cannot thrive unless you love what you do. Your ministry cannot grow unless you have love for people.

For so long love has been marketed as this mushy kind of feeling set aside for one day when you buy red heart-shaped boxes of chocolate. The reality is that love is anything but mushy.

Why?

Love is a powerful emotion. It takes courage to love. It takes determination to love. It takes fearlessness to love.

Love is the powerful glue that binds humanity. It binds us as spouses, as family, as co-workers, and anytime we join together for a common cause. It is important that you understand God's love for you. It will give you a greater love of self. Your tank must be full. It is impossible to give anything of yourself if you feel empty inside and emotionally bankrupt.

If you understand love, you put yourself in a position of power. If you have nothing against anyone and if no one can make you feel inadequate then you are free from the manipulations of others. All that is left is the ability to love others. Being able to live out love in this manner is true freedom. Love is the curtain rod upon which everything else hangs. If you are deficient in love, it will be impossible for you to have wholeness in your life.

Anything you do powered by love will allow you to succeed. If you strive to be a man of excellence, be assured that you will be challenged every step of the way to settle for being mediocre. One thing is for sure; you already have everything within you to succeed at being a man of integrity. God never asks you to do something he doesn't equip you for; you are equipped because God has deposited his love in you.

Forgiveness

It is extremely difficult to forgive without love. Forgiveness is a gift you give to yourself. Forgiveness gets you out of the prison of anger and pain. It does not mean that you are letting the other person get away with hurting you. It means that you are choosing not to be manipulated by what he or she did. In this world you will have many chances to be offended. On top of already being hurt, keeping the un-forgiveness just keeps the pain churning inside of you - sometimes for years, sometimes for a lifetime. Your life is precious. Don't let someone steal it little at a time by harboring un-forgiveness. Don't remain a victim that is not a position of power. Don't stay stuck.

Make sure your forgiveness is freely given. It should not be conditional. If you say I'll forgive when they apologize to me, then you are not forgiving. You may never get the apology you are expecting. Don't wait for it. Waiting will only increase your anger.

Why?

Forgiveness is one of the hardest things to do. It is also one of the most liberating things to do. It is the path to freedom. I learned the hard way that not forgiving ties up the person who is holding the resentment. The one who doesn't forgive is the one who ends up with the pain, the rage, and the ulcer.

How do you arrive at forgiveness? Examine your heart. Who are you angry at? Am I angry at my parents? My spouse? My children? My best friend? At a high school rival? How many years will you continue to carry the grudge? Sometimes the people who hurt you don't even know it. Sometimes they don't even care or remember what happened.

Put yourself in the other person's shoes. Ask yourself: What pain is my enemy carrying? Have I caused any of that pain? What drives this person to be so sad, so angry? When you ask these questions, you will find compassion for the other person and the path to forgiveness.

> *Ask God for help. He is our source for power, strength, and victory in every area of our lives.*

Keep in mind that forgiveness is a two-way street. Ask others for forgiveness for any harm you may have caused, whether on purpose or inadvertently. Ask God for help. He is our source for power, strength, and victory in every area of our lives. Take the challenge to forgive and take your first steps to be free.

Patience

Most people think patience means waiting. Patience actually is the ability to stay steady no matter what adversity comes your way. It is to consistently and continuously seek after your goal. How you act while you are waiting is crucial. Patience involves waiting with a good attitude. Being patient can be tough. One thing about patience that I have discovered is that it is developed. Patience is like a muscle. The more you exercise it the stronger you get. It won't come in a moment; it will come by doing it over and over again. The more adversity you face, the easier it will be to overcome. You become stronger with consistency; no longer can people get under your skin. Patience leads to greater freedom.

Life Killers:

Fear

Fear at its very core will stop you from doing what you were always meant to do. Fear will lead you to a life you were never

Why?

meant to live. Fear is the opposite of faith. There is good and evil, light and darkness. Fear is darkness. Fear will lead you down the path of destruction. Faith will lead you down the path of victory. It is you who chooses. You have been created in God's image. You are created to be a reflection of the power, the love, and the mind of God. Fear is nothing more than the thought that things will turn out wrong rather than right. It is easy to convince yourself of anything. This is why it is important to feed your brain good food, the food that gives life. What does that mean in practical terms? That means that you listen to positive podcasts like *The Good Life Project*. You listen to *Ted Talks*. You read good books like *Chicken Soup for the Soul* by Jack Canfield. You surround yourself with people who encourage you and don't squash you. You keep words in your mouth that transform and develop you into a can-do attitude versus a defeated attitude. Any man of success will tell you that success begins in the mind. Quit happens way before something ends. In the same way, winning happens way before you've finished the race.

Don't ever give in to fear. Never make decisions based on fear. Don't let past hurts drag you into fear.

Chapter 4 – Love

"For God did not give us a spirit of fear. He gave us a spirit of power and of love and of a good mind" (2 Timothy 1:7 NLV)

Don't create a life or a lifestyle centered on fear. Fear is self-perpetuating and it unravels into destruction. Run from fear and walk in confidence. You don't have to be afraid because God promises to be with you always.

"I will be with you…I will not leave you or abandon you." (Joshua 1:5 NLT)

Fear is the most useless of all emotions. A life full of fear is a life in bondage. Fear is like a bully always pushing you around telling you what to do. When you are there. Stop. Breathe. Think of the things you are grateful for. Affirm positive things in your life. I am capable. I am courageous. I am worthy. I am creative. I am talented. I am valuable. I am significant. I am accepted. I am not average, not mediocre. I am everything I was created to be. Take a moment to change your thinking. Disrupt the negative talk. Take a walk. Do something else. Do whatever you can but don't stay inside your head. A life without fear is a life of freedom. Choose to be free. Live your days in freedom.

Why?

It seems perhaps a little simplistic to say choose to be free. I know it won't always be as simple as that, but I also know that it has to be as simple as that. There will be times when you will struggle. There will be times when you feel trapped and feel like there is no way out. There will be times when you know what your choice should be and you will still feel paralyzed. At those times you have to get some grit and ask God to give you, feet to walk and wings to fly. In our own power we can stay stuck indefinitely.

> "There is no fear in Love, but perfect love casts out fear, because fear involves torment. But he who fears has not been made perfect in Love" (1 John 4:18 NIV)

You may say to yourself, *I can get myself out of this, I don't need God.* When you say those words, it will be the time you need Him the most. If you run from God, you will soon be back to the feeling of being lost and devastated. When you run to God, when you run to perfect Love, He will protect you and guide you. You will have to choose to sink or swim; to live in bondage or to be free. Freedom is a magnificent gift of life.

Chapter 4 – Love

Anger

Anger is nothing more than fear. Shocking, isn't it? Anger can manifest itself in so many ways namely: as righting a wrong, as a fight for justice. It can seem noble but that is deception. It is nothing more than fear. Fear of getting hurt. Fear of being rejected. Fear of being used. Fear of being lied to. Fear of being wrongfully accused. Fear of living in hopelessness. Fear of lack. Fear of being abandoned. Fear of stagnation. Fear of_____ you fill in the blank. Anger is just another face for fear. Because you can feel justified in your anger. Because you can feel that you have a right to your anger. This is why it is so difficult to carve it out of your life. Be very careful and very aware. Awareness is your map to freedom.

Insecurity

Insecurity is poison. It poisons your life and the lives of others, especially those who are closest to you. Insecurity makes you settle for less in every area of your life, whether it be your job, sports, hobbies, friendships, or marriage. Insecurity is very unattractive. There is nothing more attractive than a secure man. Your security will attract people. People want to know what makes you so confident.

Why?

One of the most important keys to confidence is love. Knowing that you are loved makes you confident. When you know that you are loved by your Creator it's a game changer. When you love yourself, you have strength. There is nothing more powerful than what you believe about yourself. Healthy self-love makes it possible for you to live a rich full life. Self-love comes from within. It is not determined by any outside influences. Start by seeing yourself the way your Creator sees you; it will absolutely change your perspective. What does He see you ask? He sees a masterpiece. He sees someone who is perfectly woven into the fabric of humanity. Someone with purpose and light.

Here is the big question: do you feel loved? For many of us we feel love by what people do or say and that is to be expected. However, people express their love in different ways. It is important that you understand that people have different love languages. They are words of affirmation, gifts, acts of service, quality time, and physical touch. This concept is outlined in Gary Chapman's book *The Five Love Languages*. Why am I bringing this up? The reason is because sometimes one person may be speaking in one language and you are speaking in another and you are simply not understanding what the other is saying.

Chapter 4 – Love

Your love language may be kind words. When someone talks to you nicely you receive it as love. But if that person gives you a gift and that's not your language, it really doesn't say anything to you. Get the idea? All I am saying is that you need to be careful on how you interpret that love language. Love may be shown through words, or gifts, or by serving others or simply by spending time together. What tends to happen is that people are giving away love in the way that they want to receive it. Just be aware of this dynamic. I would hate for you to feel like you are not loved and have that damage your confidence when the reality is that the other person is speaking a language you don't understand. What love language are you hearing? Some people don't even know how to express love because they have never experienced it, or because they have built walls, or because they don't love themselves. Do not get caught up in someone else's insecurity. Don't make it yours: it doesn't belong to you.

Why?

Mom's Advice:	Give and receive love with an open heart. Forgive.
Key Point:	Love is one of life's greatest gifts; don't let it pass you by because of fear.
Guiding Principle:	"Love never fades out or becomes obsolete or comes to an end" (1 Corinthians 13: 1-13 NLT)
Recommended Resources:	On communicating love: *The Five Love Languages* by Gary Chapman On forgiveness: *Let it go* by Bishop TD Jakes On Positive living: *The Good Life Project* podcast https://www.goodlifeproject.com/podcast

Chapter 4 – Love

Notes:

CHAPTER FIVE

Fatherhood

Question: How can I be a good husband and father?

What is in it for me? You will have peace and joy when you are happy as a man, husband, and father.

Why am I telling you this?
You will do things in your life that have value for a short period of time, but being a good husband and father have value not just for you but also for your children and grandchildren. It is the best gift you can give to yourself and to your family.

The Back Story
James was broken. Most of his life he felt like a failure. His mom and dad had gotten a divorce. He lived with his mom and he missed out on having a male figure in his life. He was a lonely young man. He had to go through his teenage years on his own. No one to teach him how to shave or fix a flat tire on a car. He

Why?

resented his mother because he felt his parents just hadn't tried hard enough to fix their marriage. He was angry at the way things have turned out. He felt as if his mother had robbed him of his father. He became a loner. He figured if he stayed out of people's way no one would have anything to gripe about. And if they didn't have anything to complain about, then he didn't have to feel rotten about himself. He had decided to check out of life. He retreated. He focused on his hobbies and stayed in his own little world. It was the one place he felt safe, in the one place where he felt special. It was a way not to feel the pain of not having his dad by his side. Even though James and his father saw each other on the weekends, it simply wasn't enough or the same as having him under the same roof. James figured if he didn't expect much out of life that he couldn't be hurt when he was disappointed. James carried a hole in his heart for many years. He had a hard time opening up to people. When he got to college, he met a young woman who made him feel special. She was loving and kind and very encouraging. She believed in him. She saw the many gifts and talents that he had. She saw things in him that he didn't even see in himself. James didn't think he had much to offer anyone. Whenever James would go

Chapter 5 – Fatherhood

out with his girlfriend, Allison, he would withdraw and wanted to leave whatever function they were at. In a way he abandoned Allison the way he felt he had been abandoned. This behavior started creating issues between the two of them. James would often get into fits of jealousy whenever anyone spoke to Allison. He felt threatened. Deep down, he felt as if he'd be cheated out of his time with her. Because he never opened up to Allison, she could not understand his lack of trust in her. Unspoken feelings led to poor communication and eventually led to a breakup. The breakup was just proof to James that everyone walks away.

Understand being a husband

Ideally both husband and wife share the responsibility for a marriage. Often times, it is the woman who is more focused on the health of the relationship. Believe it or not, the person with the primary responsibility for a marriage is the man. It is very important that a man understand what his role is in marriage. There used to be a time when being the man of the house meant something. The man was the protector, the leader of his home, and the guardian of his wife and children. It is instinctual for a man to be a leader. However, there is a difference between being a leader and a tyrant and that is where a lot of the pain in many

Why?

families has come in. A leader is fair; he works in peace and always looks for the good of all of those he loves. Being the man of the house carries with it a great deal of responsibility because it is the man who should deal in wisdom, honesty, integrity, faithfulness, and love. The Bible says that a man should do all good work as if he is doing it for God. It's a simple question: Would I treat God with disrespect? Would I yell at God? Would I demand from God? If you wouldn't do that with God, then why would you think it's okay for you to do it with your family?

A man trains for business, for sports, but rarely trains for his family. You wouldn't run any other race without preparing, so why would you try to lead your family without any knowledge of what your wife and children need? A man needs to gain intelligent knowledge on how to lead his family. Sometimes, the man needs to be talked into going to a seminar or seeking help. The man needs to be involved in order to be at his best for his family.

It is the need of every human being to feel accepted, important, to be secure, and to have a purpose. The man plays a crucial part in securing that all these needs are fulfilled for his family.

If you never had any of these yourself, all the more reason to study and to understand where you are first before you lead.

How? What does that look like? It is important to be real with yourself. Take inventory of your qualities. Examine your shortcomings. Clean up your side of the street by asking "how can I do better?" If you are stumped and don't know where to begin, ask questions. Look for resources or mentors to guide you. Sometimes that might simply be a book or perhaps a therapist. Whatever it is, take ownership of it and be accountable for your stuff.

The greatest needs of a man in a marriage are companionship and respect. However, it is not a given that you will automatically get the things that you need after you say "I do." You have to give to receive. You must plant the seed in order to get the harvest. The truth is that you must give affection. The more affection you show toward your wife, the more you will have a wife who gives you what you need. If your heart is empty of love, you can't give away what you don't have. Being a husband means truly giving your life for your spouse and that would include even times when you are getting nothing in return and

Why?

even when your spouse doesn't deserve it. I want to be clear; this does not mean that you become someone's doormat. What I am speaking of here is going above and beyond as long as it is not dishonoring to you.

The measure of a man is in the strength of his character and the expression of selfless love. It takes more courage to stand for these beliefs than it does to follow the crowd. In the end every man needs to make a decision of quality. That decision of quality will ultimately give you a life of quality where you benefit from the love and devotion of your family. Ultimately it is you, who receives a place of honor.

Reflecting God's Love

In God's design, the man is to be the reflection of God and his love. The woman is a reflection of the man. If a woman is always angry or sad it often is a reflection of how she is being treated at home. It is a reflection of the love or lack of love she is receiving from her husband.

Man is commanded by God to love his wife because women function on love. Ask yourself, "What is my wife reflecting?"

Chapter 5 – Fatherhood

If you don't like what you see, ask yourself where you can improve and turn things around.

Understand the definition of a father

I looked up the definition of "father" in the dictionary and it gave many different meanings for the word. The definitions that stood out for me were that a father is a man who accepts responsibility, who gives guidance, protection, and raises a child. A father is a lot more than just the biological parent. A father is an extremely important person in the life of a child. Never underestimate the importance of a father no matter what the world tells you. A father's importance has been downgraded by society. There are tons of statistics that point to fatherlessness as one of the prime contributors to crimes and societal problems. Being a father is the most important calling in a man's life. Of course, I understand that not every man will be a father. Being a father is not so much about the biological connection with a child but more about the practice of disinterested and selfless concern for the well-being of others. Nothing will ever be more gratifying than that.

Why?

Life Builders:

Have your priorities in order

Don't be a man without priorities. Have your priorities in order. Make sure that you keep a healthy balance. Having your priorities out of order will make your life a mess. When setting your priorities, make sure that you do so by considering the things that give you the maximum yield. Set your priorities by the things that are lasting, not by the things that are fleeting. The order should be God, spouse, children, and work. The order these days usually looks something like work, children, marriage, God. Of course, there is something to be said about working to provide for your family, that is not a bad thing as long as there is balance. Out of balance priorities can tend to negatively affect the relationships that are the most lasting. I guess people figure that God and the spouse are going to be around forever, so let's just put those on the back burner.

Children eventually leave home. Jobs come and go. Where are your priorities? What are you doing to set them right? As the man, you set the tone for your life and that of your family, so it is imperative that you get it right. It is not just your life you're dealing with, but the lives of others as well.

Chapter 5 – Fatherhood

Be accountable. Be responsible.

Never pawn off your responsibilities on someone else. It is not your mother-in-law's job to help with the kids. It is yours. It is not your wife's girlfriend's responsibility to help her with a project that is important to your wife – it is yours. It is not your son's responsibility to always clean the yard – it is yours. It is not your wife's sole responsibility to take care of the house, the bills, and the children – this is a shared responsibility. It is up to you as the man of the house to do what you say you are going to do. Don't make false promises to your wife or family. That is the quickest way to lose your family's confidence in you. A man who honors his word is admired. If you have agreed to have children, make yourself available to raise them too. Don't put it off just because you are afraid of the changes that a child will bring. A child is always a blessing and brings great reward to the man who makes the investment.

Always keep your end of a deal. Having integrity will make you a success, not only in your relationship but in your work. Stick it out. Half the battle is just hanging in there. Don't quit at the first sign of trouble. Trouble is to be expected. Trouble is part of learning. Trouble is what teaches you to be stronger. Trouble

Why?

shows you the pitfalls so that your success comes quicker the next time. If you do something wrong, remember that you are accountable to your wife and family. You cannot just quit and fail your family and not be accountable. When you are given great gifts, they require great responsibility. Don't run; you are a strong man and you are up to the task.

Humility

The greatest position of power is on your knees. If you are too proud to assume a posture of humility, you will effectively block your ability to get wisdom regarding the challenges you may be facing. When you are in a situation where you see no way out, when you are in a situation where you don't know what to do, the only one that knows the perfect answer is God. Before Jesus was going to go to the cross, he got on his knees. Only by being on his knees was he able to get the strength and the courage to carry out God's perfect plan for humanity. He became the perfect gift to us. Because he is our perfect gift, this is why today we can come to him with our problems and know that we will find a way out. If you are too proud to apologize for a wrong, you risk your relationships. Say you are sorry to your father, your sister, your friend, your mother. Your life will be more fulfilled and brimming with love when you are willing to give up your arrogance. Don't be a snob. Everything and everyone have value. Corruption of this value is why the world labels people as "losers." This

> *Being confident in yourself will make you confident in your relationships.*

is like a lottery ticket. You may have been nurtured and your life turned out to be one of excellence. You may not have been nurtured and your life turned out to be nothing but pain. Thank God for his mercy. Thank him that you got lucky.

> "A man's pride and sense of self-importance will bring him down, but he who has a humble spirit will obtain honor"
>
> (Proverbs 29:23 AMP)

Just because you got a break should not be a justification for arrogance. Arrogance has various expressions: criticism, impatience, judgment, hatred, and selfishness. Check yourself. When you see any of these expressions, you'll know that you are walking in arrogance. You are not doing yourself any favors. This is the quickest way to get into isolation and despair. You can avoid a lot of trouble by avoiding arrogance.

Why?

Life Killers:

Obsession

Here is a tricky one; matters of the heart. It is at the core of our humanity. We were made to love. So much has been done and said in the name of love. It is such a powerful emotion. Sometimes without even thinking it can carry you away to places you never thought you'd end up in. Be careful not to allow any one relationship to be your obsession. Don't make pleasing your parents a sickly obsession. Don't make pleasing your spouse a frustrating goal. Don't make pleasing a friend your main thing. Remember that balance is the key. Don't go too far into one extreme or the other. Realize that what you are really seeking is acceptance. Make sure you accept yourself first. And know that you are fully accepted by God just the way you are, flaws and all.

Being confident in yourself will make you confident in your relationships. Sometimes, it is the most difficult relationships that make you grow the most. Sometimes you can give so much of yourself in a relationship that you lose who you are. It is not wrong to want good relationships, but when your happiness is

Chapter 5 – Fatherhood

centered on what other people do then you are in trouble. You need to have peace and joy with yourself.

If others are being unkind, unreasonable, selfish, irresponsible, or whatever it shouldn't affect your peace or joy. No one can go for that kind of a roller coaster ride for too long and survive. Sometimes you'll have lifetime relationships that you think you just can't walk away from, so you need to learn to survive them and realize that you are dealing with imperfect people.

Being a control freak

Being a control freak is nothing more than fear. It is a desperate attempt to control another's actions and your circumstances. You know for sure you can't control others, and as far as your circumstances you might be able to control them maybe for a little while. It takes a great deal of effort to control everything. You will be mentally and physically exhausted. You can't make people fit into your vision of who they should be. You can't make them do what you want so that you can be happy or feel safe. People were never meant to be manipulated. When you attempt to manipulate others, it often breeds resentment, and in the end, you bear the cost—through isolation and the loss

Why?

of genuine connection. Instead of achieving the closeness you desire you push them away. Your strength should come from within, not from people or things. That is a recipe for disaster. You will always be disappointed. You have to get at the root of your fear. Fear implies punishment for something. Giving in to fear is like saying I deserve the punishment. Identify your fears and work on them one by one. Do what you have to do to get help. For some people that means that they talk to a friend or see a therapist or even go to a pastor but the main person to seek out here is God. You have to get to know the love that God has for you. His love will take away the fear. Perfect love always casts out fear. Give yourself a chance to be free.

Rejection

Rejection is like being on the wrong side of the lake. It's being able to see the other side but convincing yourself that you can't make it there. It's telling yourself why bother because no one cares if you are there or not. Rejection is

> *The more you shy away from people because you think they will reject you, the more they will.*

deceptive. Rejection is a self-perpetuating fear. The more you shy away from people because you think they will reject you,

Chapter 5 – Fatherhood

the more they will. People in general are attracted to dynamic people. If you don't demonstrate that you are approachable, then why would anyone approach you? They may be just as afraid as you are to make the first step and someone will have to.

Sometimes rejection though, goes beyond social rejection. Sometimes rejection comes from people who are close to you. When that happens, there are usually two reasons: they are either not comfortable with themselves or they are jealous of you. It is especially difficult when that comes from a family member because family is supposed to accept you the most. But I have found that sometimes parents and siblings can sometimes be carrying a load that they just do not know how to let go of.

Remember, as people we tend to be very complex. Most people hide their wounds deep inside, or determine that they will never be wounded again. When a father has a hard time getting close to his son it's usually because he's carrying such pain inside that he does not even now where to begin. Some dads have lacked a role model and haven't learned how to open up to their children. Sooner or later, somebody has to make the decision of not letting the pain get in the way. Sometimes it's not the parent. If we have

Why?

been given a life, it is our privilege and our honor to live it the best way we can. You can't wait for everyone else to make the first move. You have to save yourself from the destructive power of rejection. Even though you may not see yourself as special, someone else probably recognizes your talent and hopes that you'll never smarten up and recognize yourself. As long as you have low self-esteem, you can stay on your side of the lake and never come to the other side to claim what was always for you. Rejection is nothing more than a manipulating force that keeps you living below where you were meant to. It leads to a life of frustration and un-fulfillment. And no one can go at it like that for an undetermined amount of time without some damage. Make sure that you are not the person who becomes destroyed by this behavior.

Chapter 5 – Fatherhood

Mom's Advice: Listen to your wife and children, respect and love them.

Key Point: Families need a guide, especially boys, so be available to them.

Guiding Principle: "Fathers, do not aggravate your children, or they will become discouraged" (Colossians 3:21 NLT)

Recommended Resources:

On relationships: *Love, Sex, and Lasting Relationships* by Chip Ingram

On loving your wife: *The Love Dare* by Alex Kendrick

On discipline for children: *Have a New Kid by Friday* by Kevin Leman

On family life: *The Successful Family: Everything you need to know to build a stronger Family* by Creflo Dollar

On family life: *The Vintage Family* by Drenda Keesee

Why?

Notes:

CHAPTER SIX

Marriage

Question: How do I know she's Mrs. Right?

What is in it for me? Happiness.

Why am I telling you this?

Choosing the right person to live your life with is critical. Make sure she is an asset and not a liability. Choosing the wrong person can drag you down and rob you of time, money, energy, and dreams.

The Back Story:

There are a lot of stories about lives being destroyed. Some are obvious and some are silent killers. Adam married a girl who was addicted to drugs. She even took them while she was pregnant. The result was their baby was born with brain damage. Tina left her husband after having five children with him to marry a guy half her age. Susan spent all her time at clubs and gambling and ended up neglecting her kids and losing a ton of money.

Why?

Those are the women with the flashing neon signs. The ones to be most careful of are the ones that appear to be o.k. Maria was a nice girl, a little broken due to her dad leaving at an early age and being abused but still a nice girl. She went to school, helped her mom out, and wanted to get married. The unfortunate thing was that she was critical, judgmental, insecure, unforgiving, and controlling.

After nearly 40 years of marriage, Jose was beaten. He had enough. Maria disapproved of the choices her daughter Elena made. At the core of it, she was angry that she had no control. It got to the point that she wouldn't allow her husband or the rest of the family to communicate with Elena. This went on for years. Maria kept her entire family hostage to her anger and disappointment. She alienated her daughter and denied herself the opportunity to be with her grandchildren. Women come from all walks of life with different stories. Watch out for the flashing neon signs and watch out for the subtle ones too.

How do you know she's the one?

You need to figure out if it's love or infatuation. Test your feelings. Here are a few tests that can tell you whether she is the one for you. These tests come from Chip Ingram's book *Love Sex*

Chapter 6 – Marriage

and Lasting Relationship. The tests are Chip's but the explanations are mine.

Ingram, Chip. "How to know if you are in love" *Love, sex, and Lasting Relationships*, Baker Books, 2003. pp.87-103.

The test of time

Love at first sight? Hmm, not so much. That only happens in movies. It's a fantasy. She's hot. She is gorgeous, sexy, and sweet. She might be scrumptious. It's just like looking at a dessert tray, it might be the best-looking dessert you have ever seen but it doesn't mean it's good for you. Give your relationship time. How can you say that you can't live without her when you've only known her for a couple of months? You were living just fine without her two months ago. Take the time to know her. Find out about her thoughts and attitudes. Ask questions. Is she jealous? Is she controlling? Is she materialistic? Is she a train wreck? Is she jaded and guarded? Be still, give it time, don't make any rush decisions. If it's the real deal she'll be there for you no matter how much time passes. Does she fulfill the things you are looking for? If the answer is "yes," she may be the one. Is she someone worth waiting for? Love grows with time. Infatuation comes on suddenly.

Why?

The test of knowledge

When you go for a job a background check is usually done. Employers look at your credit report. Companies have you take a physical or a drug test. Some businesses have you do a personality assessment. They check your driver's license. If people agree to all of this for a job, why would you not do the same for someone you are about to share your life with? This is a two-way street. Look into what she brings to the table. Look at yourself as well. Does it sound paranoid? Maybe. Things have changed. Today people meet over the internet. You may not necessarily start a relationship with someone you have known all your life – like a friend from school. Since both of you may be coming together from very different places, it is important to get to know as much as possible about the other person. Ask questions. Does she have a job? Does she want one? Does she want to stay home and raise her kids? Does she have any kids from a previous relationship? Are you willing to step in and become a father to those children? When it is love, it grows out of knowing all aspects of the person. If it's infatuation, it is usually based on knowing just a few things about the individual.

How well do you know your fiancée or spouse? Has she shared

her dreams with you? Do you want to be a part of those dreams? Do you want to support those dreams? Who will take care of the home and children while you pursue your ambitions? Find out and then decide.

The test of focus

Love is "other person" focused. Are you willing to give her preferential treatment? Do you put her needs above your own? Are you her friend? Is she yours? Can you both reach a compromise or are you both selfish? Do you treat her like a lady? Do you want to? Do you know what that means? It comes down to treating her with respect. That means you don't do, say or otherwise imply anything that can be sexually offensive. You don't use sexually charged words, you don't show her pornographic material, you don't make crude jokes. Do you want her? Or do you want something from her?

> *When it is love, it grows out of knowing all aspects of the person. If it's infatuation, it is usually based on knowing just a few things about the individual.*

When it is love, the other person is focused on you. When it's infatuation the other person is self-centered. If you go into a relationship focused on what's in it for you, eventually you will lose. As soon as she doesn't meet your expectations, you will be disappointed. If you go into it prepared to give, you will receive. Remember it's a two-way street. You have to look at it from both angles.

The test of singularity

Is she the only one you want to be with? Or are you greedy? Do you want more than one woman? Are you confident she's the one you want, or are you wishy washy? As I always like to say if it's not a "heck yeah," it's a "heck no." Do you want to bring her to meet your parents? If you are not serious about her, then don't bring her to meet the family. Do you introduce her as your girlfriend or do you say she is only a friend? If so, that tells you that you are not so serious about her.

Being unable to commit to one person. That is fear. That is not love. The Bible says that perfect love drives out fear. It also says that a person who fears has not seen love's perfection. If you love her, you will profess your love for her. You will provide for and protect her. Are you ready to do that?

Let's go a little further. What does keeping your individuality look like once you are married? What happens when you are exhausted from dealing with the kids, financial pressure, a demanding job, or loneliness? Life can get hard, monotonous, and love in marriage can get cold. "One of the side effects of stale times in marriage is vulnerability to infatuation.... When feelings have temporarily dried up from one direction, it's hard not to pay attention to feelings coming from another direction.... The great majority of affairs rarely occur solely on the basis of physical attraction. They usually start out with a little chemistry during times of vulnerability. But families break up because very good, godly people have not learned what to do in these situations. They confuse infatuation with love and make foolish decisions. The cycle of infatuation is nine to eighteen months. Then all those breathless and wonderful feelings leave, and you're stuck with another person with the same kinds of needs that you have. That person knows you can't be trusted because you left your last mate. You know you can't really trust them because, down deep, you're afraid of experiencing the kind of betrayal you inflicted on someone else. What's left are two unhappy people struggling with character flaws."

Ingram, Chip. "How to know if you are in love" *Love, sex, and Lasting Relationships*, Baker Books, 2003. P.96

Why?

The test of security

Are you secure in the relationship? Does she crave an inordinate amount of male attention? Can other females trust her around their mates? Is she insecure? Is that why she needs the attention? Does she have an abnormal appetite for sex? Does she respect men or just use them? Can you trust her? Is she really the kind of woman you want to marry?

When love is real you trust. You know the person's character and values and because she has a proven track record; you can trust. If there is jealousy that is a sign of a lack of trust. A lack of trust is a sign of infatuation. Or it can be a sign that the other person is guilty of fooling around behind your back. Either way, open your eyes. Don't ignore the signs. How secure are you in the relationship?

The test of work

Are you willing to work for her? Do you put your whole heart into providing the best for her? If a man really loves a woman, he doesn't mind going out there and getting a job. He doesn't mind putting in the effort to make her life a little easier. He doesn't mind giving of himself for her comfort. Or do you say you are

Chapter 6 – Marriage

going to get a job but don't even fill out an application? Do you call yourself an "entrepreneur" or an "artist" but have no real plans or prospects to back that up? Conversely, is she willing to do her part and support you in your efforts to provide? Or is she lazy? Does she have an attitude of entitlement?

They say that love is blind, but it can't be because love always sees clearly. If you are the kind of man who is willing to put sweat equity into building a future with a woman, then she may be, the one. The question here is are you both willing to put in the effort to build a future together? If you both build it together, then it is love. If you are both floating in a cloud, it is infatuation. That is not a strong foundation to build on.

The test of problem solving

How do you resolve problems? If you say to yourself "oh we never fight," "we're okay." You are deceiving yourself. Just by virtue of the fact that you are a man and she is a woman you will have some conflict at some point. Men and women see the world differently. How will both of you face the challenges that are sure to be ahead of you? As long as you are living you will face problems. Do you manage it in a productive manner or

Why?

does it turn into a shouting match? Do you both sacrifice and come to a solution that is fair? Do you come to an agreement without blaming one another for one thing or another? Do you speak to each other in love or in anger? This is a very important aspect of a relationship. The way you solve problems can either build or destroy your relationship. People who are in love face the hard issues. People who are infatuated just think that everything is going to magically work out. What obstacles do you and your mate feel positive about facing and overcoming in your relationship?

The test of distance

Is the love stronger when you are together and weaker when you are not? Real love is more consistent. Infatuation varies depending on the distance or the circumstances. Are you still communicating with one another despite the distance? Are you still concerned with each other's well-being, goals, and plans? Does the distance make your bond stronger or weaker? Is the person faithful to you even with the distance? Or does the individual see this as a prime opportunity to do whatever she wants? Perhaps thinking along the lines of "what you don't know won't hurt you." Distance can be an asset to you. A little time away from each other can help determine whether you still feel as passionate about her as you did initially. How does she feel about you after some time has passed? This can reveal whether there are any gaps in your relationship. Does she need to be with you every waking moment? Is she clingy? Does she want you all to herself? Infatuation usually needs the other person 24/7 or she will "just die" without you. That's just not healthy or sustainable. Have you spent time apart? What did you learn?

The test of physical attraction

When a couple is in love the physical attraction is just but one part of the relationship. It is not more important or significant than the other parts. When it is infatuation, the physical attraction is everything. Having one pleasurable experience after another is the focus. It's like being addicted to a drug: you just have to have it. It is usually centered on pleasurable physical contact without any depth or real meaning. Will you still be physically attracted to her when she is sick? When she is having a bad day? When something tragic happens will you still be there? Or are you only there for the good times? What does she do when you are down and out? How does she behave when you need her? Is she

Why?

the kind of person you would want in your life? Think about it.

The test of affection

When someone is in love, affection comes a lot later in the relationship. When the person is infatuated, affection comes very early on even in the beginning. While it may feel good to have someone's attention, beware. Is this person genuine? Is this person "in love with love?" Is this person looking for a real relationship? Or is the affection a tool that is used to get intimate with you? I am not suggesting that you have to be paranoid, but you do have to be of sober mind. You need to look at the other person's motives. Take your time to evaluate. It is best not to rush into anything or get swept up by the moment. When you do, it can have very negative consequences with a high price tag. It can cost you time, emotional torment, money, self-esteem, and a host of other things. Proceed with caution. Make sure that affection is balanced out by genuine friendship. Make sure that there is a willingness to give and that a selfish want is not the ultimate reason for getting close to you. It's almost like saying guilty until proven innocent. Look at her and yourself in this area.

Chapter 6 – Marriage

The test of stability

Does the person you are in relationship with tend to be unstable? Does she change suddenly? Is she unpredictable? Is she unreliable? Do her feelings go hot to cold very quickly? Is she in love with you today and not so much tomorrow? Is she in love with you and maybe another person at the same time? If the answer to any of these questions is "yes" then it can be called infatuation. When people are confused about their feelings they are infatuated. Love tends to be stable no matter what is going on. Check her out. How are her other relationships? Is she nice to her parent? To her friends? To her siblings? The question to ask is: "What is her track record?" Are there toxic patterns that send warning signals? How do you feel about being with someone like that? Are you stable with her? Be a careful observer.

The test of delayed gratification

The question here is can both of you wait? Are you rushing to the altar? Does the thought of waiting seem unbearable to both of you? Do you feel a sense of agony and desperation? If so, you are probably infatuated. Can you wait a reasonable time? Do you take things in stride? Do you postpone your union in marriage until you are clear about things that matter, such as being clear

121

about shared values? If so, then probably you are in love. Do a gut check. Do you feel comfortable? Do you have reservations? If so, take some time to get clarity. Delayed gratification will be worth it in the end.

These tests will give you a better picture of where you stand. They can also guide you to make a wise decision. In the end, they will save you a lot of headaches, heartaches, disappointments, and pain.

How did you do in the tests? Did you find that maybe you are not as "in love" as you thought? Did you discover that you are more infatuated? Pause and think. Is this really what I want? Will I settle for a cheap copy of love or hold out for the real deal? My hope is that you will make wise choices.

Life Builders:

Be "all in"

When you decide to get married, you claim responsibility for your spouse. You are taking on the responsibility to protect and care for her. Marriage is the ultimate expression of sacrificial love. This kind of love decides to stand by someone no matter

Chapter 6 – Marriage

what happens; this is huge! I don't want you to be afraid of commitment because God is well able to equip you with all that you will need to be successful in marriage. It is important, however, to be careful of what you claim as your own. As my grandmother used to say: "not everything that shines is gold." You can be attracted to a woman who looks like a supermodel who might be bi-polar, anorexic, angry, etc. I am not suggesting that someone who has these issues is someone who is unworthy of being loved; please do not misunderstand. What I am saying is that you should investigate before you invest. Make sure that if there are challenges you are prepared to meet those challenges. Don't be surprised by them and then run, because that can cause more damage than letting go from the beginning. I am not trying to choose the woman you will marry, either. The choice is yours. However, there are some qualities that are worth considering when you are choosing the woman who will be your life partner. Is she whole? Does she have a sense of her worth? If she is spiritual, does she see God as her source of love? If a woman relies on God for her peace and joy, she is complete in GOD. This is crucial because a woman who knows who she is will not place unrealistic expectations on you to

Why?

fulfill her innermost needs. If she feels whole then she can give you the very best she has to offer without fear or reservation. A good woman can make an average man great. This is not mom's version of what a wife should look like, this is God's version of what to look for.

Choose a Proverbs 31 Woman

"If you can find a truly good wife, she is worth more than precious gems! Her husband can trust her, and she will richly satisfy his needs. She will not hinder him but help him all her life. She finds wool and flax and busily spins it. She buys imported foods brought by ship from distant ports. She gets up before dawn to prepare breakfast for her household and plans the day's work for her servant girls. She goes out to inspect a field and buys it; with her own hands she plants a vineyard. She is energetic, a hard worker, and watches for bargains. She works far into the night!

She sews for the poor and generously helps those in need. She has no fear of winter for her household, for she has made warm clothes for all of them. She also upholsters with finest tapestry; her own clothing is beautifully made—a purple gown of pure linen. Her husband is well known, for he sits in the council chamber with the other civic leaders. She makes belted linen garments to sell to the merchants.

She is a woman of strength and dignity and has no fear of old age. When she speaks, her words are wise, and kindness is the rule for everything she says. She watches carefully all that goes on throughout her household and is never lazy. Her children stand and bless her; so does her husband. He praises her with these words: "There are many fine women in the world, but you are the best of them all!"

Charm can be deceptive and beauty doesn't last, but a woman who fears and reverences God shall be greatly praised. Praise her for the many fine things she does.

These good deeds of hers shall bring her honor and recognition from people of importance."

(Proverbs 31:10-30 TLB)

An important note here. Remember to keep expectations kind and balanced. A Proverbs 31 woman is not someone to be treated like a servant. **She is your partner.** She is the one that stands beside you, not under you or behind you. **Respect her.**

Be a complete, whole person before you get married.

Marry someone who is complete. Respect your partner's individuality and goals. Support your partner's goals. Make goals as a couple. Make goals as a family. Sharing goals, carrying each other's burdens, helping each other, builds unity.

Always exercise love first.

Do not judge, criticize, or be jealous of your partner – that is a sign

Why?

of selfishness and arrogance. There is no room for selfishness in marriage. Selfishness destroys families.

Put God at the center of your marriage. When two people are committed to doing their best for God, it is by matter of consequence that they can do better for each other. If you both love God first it will be much easier to love each other.

> *Put God at the center of your marriage*

It takes a lot of maturity and sacrifice to marry someone. Getting married doesn't necessarily mean that you are mature so it's important to be ready. This means that insecurities need to be left at the door because they are lethal to marriage. You have to be ready to give in order to marry. It's not about what you can get. Love is the root of every relationship. It is deceiving to think that passionate love is going to take you all the way in marriage. You must have the willingness to give even when you can't find a reason to do so. Love is not the hot passion you feel when you first meet. If that is your measuring stick for love, it will always disappoint you. No human being can sustain that intensity for a lifetime, much less when responsibilities for work and children come along. Make sure, however, to always make time for each other and don't use work or children or other responsibilities as an excuse to slack off. If you don't make your marriage a priority, it won't be a priority. The rewards of a good marriage, however are immeasurable. It makes you feel grounded and it also gives you wings.

Practical things to show your wife you love her
1. Give your wife of your time.
2. Listen to her.
3. Be courteous with her, show good manners.
4. Leave her notes.
5. Speak kindly to her – don't be rude.
6. Treat her with respect.
7. Give her the freedom to be who she is; don't put her in a box.

A woman's needs:
1. Emotional: romantic, flowers, smiles, winks.
2. Non-sexual touching.
3. Intimacy – share your thoughts: your wife really wants to know her husband.
4. Security – home, income, retirement.
5. Understand her needs.
6. Help around the house.
7. Time with husband.
8. Help with children.

Why?

Just as you have responsibilities so, too, does the woman. Make your needs known to your wife. Don't get out of balance. The entire family's attitude should be one of support and service. What can we all do to serve one another and help each other for the well-being of all?

A man's basic needs are:
1. Physical love – let your wife know that you would like her to take the initiative.
2. Hugs and kisses – a man needs to be showered with attention.
3. Understanding.
4. Respect – a man needs to be complimented consistently for his contributions.
5. Confidante – a man needs someone to confide in.
6. Orderly, clean home.
7. Humor.
8. Playful glances, looks, smiles, winks.

Choose the mother of your children wisely

When I was in my twenties, the only thing I looked for in a guy was that he be good looking and nice. I wish someone had told me that it was going to take more than those superficial attributes to make a successful marriage. When you're young, you think the good looks and the feelings you have for one another are all that matter because if you love each other everything else will work itself out. Sometimes even with the greatest of human love, it is impossible to succeed. I can tell you from experience that it takes God's love to carry a marriage even if you love each other madly. As you mature you find that a marriage takes trust, and you start to appreciate other qualities like integrity, work ethic, and tenacity. The person you choose as a wife and mother will be the one who will help you to establish your family on a solid foundation, so she can't be a quitter. She will be the person that shapes and molds children. She will have the awesome task of bringing up the next generation with you. Many people don't think in terms of posterity. What does that future look like? How are you and your spouse going to contribute to the well-being of you children and grandchildren? What are you planting into your family today that will help your family and others in the future? You and she are building the people for our future society. A mother must have courage, tenacity, and a generous heart.

Life Killers:

Don't live solely by your feelings
Don't make the feelings of the moment your guide. Stop. Think.

Why?

Exercise wisdom. I get it, you're probably thinking where am I supposed to get that wisdom? Doesn't that take time and come with age? Sure, some of it does but deep down you have an idea as to whether something serves you in your path of life or whether it doesn't. What I am saying is to slow it down long enough to make decisions when you are not in the heat of things. Feelings change from one moment to the next. You can't trust your feelings all the time. Don't make choices solely on how you feel at a particular moment. You may feel differently in the morning. You may feel different after your anger has subsided. You may feel different after the "newness" has worn off. You may feel different after you stop being in love with love. You may feel different when you get to know the real person. Feelings can be treacherous. They are not always your best guide.

> "The heart is the most deceitful thing there is and desperately wicked. No one can really know how bad it is!"
> (Jeremiah 17:9 TLB)

Let me give you an example. Some people are masterful at manipulating others. If someone plays on your feelings, he or she is just trying to gain whatever is important to them, no matter what the cost is to you. How can you trust your feelings

Chapter 6 – Marriage

when you are being tricked? Beware and be aware of those people who are skillful at gaining the advantage.

On the other hand, there are some people who aren't deliberately trying to hurt others. Sometimes people hurt each other without even noticing. People can be completely clueless about the stuff that comes out of their mouths. Sometimes feelings are so powerful that you can only think about the injustice that someone has put you through. If your focus is "that's just not right," "how dare they talk to me that way," "what gives them the right to act anyway they want while I do the right thing?" It is easy to get caught up in the hurt. And if you are a sensitive person like I was, mulling over words that were said in haste can cause you years of anguish. Don't make your feelings your god.

If you are constantly focused on the hurt that someone has caused you, if you are always consumed by un-forgiveness, if you feel like another person owes you, you will always come up short, because the bottom line is that other people won't be able to make up for what they did. If you are always going to the altar of your wounded feelings, of your hurt, to worship your pain and the injustices in your life, then you can never be free.

Why?

You will be stuck in un-forgiveness. You will never be able to see the good in those who have hurt you. You will never be able to grow.

If, however, you stop going to the altar of your pain, then God can heal you. People can't make you whole. Only God can make you whole. God can open your eyes to the good in others. God can also give you coping mechanisms while you go through the process and grow in the area of love. This goes back to what I mentioned earlier about the love-power connection. If you are bogged down by your disappointments, there is no way that you can walk tall to the victory that God has set apart for you. Let it go. Refuse to allow anything negative to pollute your world. Shut the door on negativity: don't let it come in and ruin the good things in your relationships. This goes for all your relationships – with your mother, brother, sister, daughter, son, spouse, etc. Don't let the bad stuff get in and keep you stuck in a life that is mediocre. God has a much better life for you. Whether you believe it or not, you can never go wrong with God. Seek the wisdom of God in everything you do.

Don't live in extremes

Balance is the key; too much of one thing or the other makes for a real bumpy ride. It's the Dr. Jekyll, Mr. Hyde thing. No one knows whether you are coming or going - not even yourself. It is very difficult to develop relationships when you are in extremes. It goes for all relationships, business or personal. It becomes hard for people to trust you because it's basically a crapshoot. It also gives the impression that you don't know whether you are coming or going. Extremes are driven by impulses, going off emotionally from one thing to the next. The problem is that emotions change, so that what makes sense this minute does not make sense the next. How can you even save face and lend credibility to the last impulse you had when you can't even justify it yourself. Be temperate. You should rule your emotions, your emotions should not rule you. Weigh your options. Listen more and talk less: this is advice that can take you a real long way, believe me. Give yourself time; things might not always be what they appear to be. Give others the benefit of the doubt and then when you have gathered all your information, act.

Why?

Mom's Advice:	Make sure you share the same values.
Key Point:	Look before you leap. This is a critical decision.
Guiding Principle:	"Not everyone is mature enough to live a married life. It requires a certain aptitude and grace. Marriage isn't for everyone. Some, from birth seemingly, never give marriage a thought. Others never get asked, or accepted. And some decide not to get married for kingdom reasons. But if you are capable of growing into the largeness of marriage, do it." (Matthew 19:11-12 MSG)
Recommended Resources:	**On marriage:** *Lies at the Altar* by Dr. Robin Smith (This book is critical before you get married – Read it! Discuss it with the person you are thinking of marrying. Look before you leap!) **On boundaries:** *Boundaries* by Dr. Henry Cloud & Dr. John Townsend (If I had only read this book sooner) **On relationships:** *Love, Sex, and Lasting Relationships* by Chip Ingram **On sex:** *Sheet Music* by Kevin Leman

Chapter 6 – Marriage

Notes:

Chapter Seven

Work

Question: What kind of work should I do?

What is in it for me? If you don't work, you don't eat.

Why am I telling you this?

Work is important in a man's life. Work is not just a way of surviving and supporting yourself; a man derives a lot of his value from his work. When I say "work," I don't necessarily mean a job. "Work" can also mean to run your own company, be an entrepreneur, or an investor. Work allows you to take control of your destiny if you know where you want to go.

The Back Story

My mom has the strongest work ethic of anyone I know. She is tireless. She does not stop until what she sets out to do is accomplished. When you are young, you hope you don't turn out like your parents and when you get older you realize that

Why?

you share lots of their traits. I used to think that was a bad thing. Sure, I am not the same as my mom, but there are some things about her that are amazing. Her work ethic is one of them. There were times when I looked at a task, and thought there is no way that I can get that done. Mom would come in and even if it was hard and even if it took extra effort she would push through until it was accomplished. I call her the miracle worker. She worked at an import/export company. I remember going to see her at the office of the World Trade Center. Her desk would be filled with client files. I saw her buried under those files and every day she woke up, she worked and chipped away at it. You don't realize the sacrifices that mothers make until you find yourself doing the same for your own family. She has been such an amazing example to me. She taught me never to quit. She taught me to have resolve in the face of adversity. She taught me that nothing is impossible. She taught be that there is no sacrifice too big for your family. I am sure that she didn't think she was doing all that, but I was watching. I learned that if I wanted something, I had to go after it.

Types of Work

As you consider what kind of work you want to do in the future,

Chapter 7 – Work

it is important to understand the different types of work that exist and what their implication is to your bottom line and your personal satisfaction.

In Robert Kiyosaki's book *Rich Dad, Poor Dad* he explains that there are four quadrants. What I got out of it is that two of these quadrants will make you poor and the other two will make you rich. In the poor quadrant are the employees and the self-employed. In the rich quadrant are the big business and the investors. I added some other types of work in this section but they are closely related to the other four.

The question then is where do you want to be? What are you willing to do to get there? (And, by the way, you can get there without doing it illegally.) And how does this work line up with your priorities?

Employees

Many people are in the employee quadrant where they trade time for money. That is what most of us have been taught. Its primary value is in getting work experience that can help you in other future endeavors. The down side is no work, no check. If you do not manage your money wisely, you can find yourself

Why?

on the street. Ultimately someone else is deciding whether you and your family get to eat. Someone else is determining how far you can go and that is a tough place to be.

Self-employed

Some people like to be the boss, so they start their own business and are self-employed. However, they don't own the business, the business owns them. They spend most of their time babysitting employees. The rest of the time they're chasing down customers or accounts receivables. They have no life. If you own a business like this, often times, your life is entirely caught up in your business. If you can't enjoy the fruits of your labor, that is really no way to live. At this point you are trading your time for money.

Big Business

Then there are those who are in big business as Robert Kiyosaki calls it. This is where you create a system and the system makes money for you. This is where you do the work once and get paid for it over and over again. This is residual income. This is very powerful. You find this kind of money in subscription services. You create a service and subscribers pay a monthly fee for that

Chapter 7 – Work

service. This is very popular these days. These businesses are often automated and outsourced requiring little of your time.

You also find this kind of money in multi-level marketing. I know it has a bad reputation because some unscrupulous people have ruined it with unethical practices and Ponzi schemes. There are some reputable ones out there and they also work on a subscription model. You can get some guidance on that by seeing which ones have a good reputation with the Direct Selling Association of America. You also want to see which ones have longevity - that says a lot about the company. Also take look at who the company is partnered with; if it has relationships with other big-name company that says a lot about what kind of company it is. I will caution you that this isn't for everyone. A very small percentage of people make it in this kind of environment. You have to have unwavering determination, focus and very thick skin. If this is not you, then don't go down this path. Many have wasted a lot of time and money for very small returns.

You can also find this kind of residual income by selling programs and systems on line. You record your words of wisdom once and

Why?

you make money over and over again because people purchase your recordings.

Creative

In the area of big business there are also the creative workers. Artists in music, film, and writing who do the work once and get paid royalties. In this field it is extremely important to get a good contract. A bad contract can leave you with debt rather than a good income even though you may be working hard at your craft. Get an experienced lawyer to review your contract. This is critical. Also don't get caught up in the hype. Being a legend in your own mind or being idolized can make you think you are invincible. Any armor gets a chink. Don't let the distractions bring you down.

Investors

This is where you send your money to work for you. One place where many people invest is the stock market. Sometimes you make money, sometimes you lose money. You have to be comfortable with that in order to win.

There are other ways to send your money to grow. You can partner in a business venture like the folks on "Shark Tank."

Chapter 7 – Work

You can invest in real estate and gain a residual income from rents. You can get a car wash or laundromat that will make you money. Did you know you can own an ATM machine and make money from the fees? You can consider a franchise. There are a variety of vehicles in this space. Always look for ways to make your money work for you.

Consider investing in cryptocurrencies. Do your research. Most people think this kind of investment is too risky or a scam. And they wouldn't necessarily be wrong. However, many governments globally have already established legislation around cryptocurrencies or are about to. My humble suggestion is that you invest in those coins that have real world applications. Invest in those that large corporate giants are investing in. Are there countries that have already passed crypto legislation? What coins are they investing in? Again, do the research to understand what is going on with the world financial system. Things are changing rapidly in the world, educate yourself and don't get left behind. Searching the Internet you will find a plethora of information.

Why?

Charitable

This is the kind of work that you will find with nonprofit organizations, foundations, and churches. These positions generally, pay a modest salary. If you are called to this kind of work, then it is especially important to budget and invest wisely. There are folks who provide trusts in order to fund the work of a charity. I know of a lady who was the recipient of such a trust and she used those funds specifically for her mission work. This was key because she did not have to dip into her own funds in order to do the work she loves. If you are called to do this work, make sure you find a charity that aligns to your values. This is critical because being in the right place will keep you motivated, passionate, and fulfilled.

Life Builders:

Success and Promotion

Here are some simple, practical things that you can do that will help you in achieving success and promotion.

1. **Take care of your appearance**

When you go for that important meeting, look your best. Why? First impressions are very important. Take pride in your appearance. People gravitate towards those who look successful. People notice when you look sharp. There is something about an elegant, well-groomed man that makes people want to follow you. Caring for your appearance demonstrates that you take pride in yourself and that you are a person of excellence. Excellence is something that people look for in others. Whether someone is looking for a business partner or an employee, excellence is quality that is sought after. Excellence is a rare jewel. Be that treasure.

2. **Show up on time**

Showing up on time is a sign of respect. It is disrespectful to waste someone's time. Someone once told me that being early is being on time. Being on time is being late and being late is never done. We should honor the time others are giving us by showing up on time. Being on time is important, not just on the day of your interview or the meeting but every day. Having a job is not a right; it is a privilege. It is your opportunity to learn so that you will gain the tools to be an effective leader in the future. If you have a job to go to it's because someone has put a lot of effort at building a successful business. Just because it's a corporation doesn't mean that there isn't a leadership team

Why?

putting in some serious effort to keep the place going. The very least you could do is show up on time. You have been entrusted with an opportunity, show up to that opportunity. Whether that opportunity is a job or a business deal, show that you value it. After all, don't you want people to be respectful of your time in the same way you are of theirs?

3. **Pay attention to details**

Pay close attention to the tasks that you have been asked to complete. Make sure you do them with care. Do your best not to miss any important details. Make a checklist for yourself. Anticipate objections and address them in your body of work. If possible, share your ideas with a trusted colleague before your official presentation. This work ethic is what business partners and employers look for in their employees and future leaders.

4. **Stay on task – finish what you start**

If you said it, do it. If you started it, finish it. If someone asks you to do something, make sure you always close the loop. You wouldn't build the foundation to a house and then not build on it, so why would you do that with your work? If you commit to something, see it through. Be a doer, not a talker. It's simple. Like Nike says *"Just do it."*

Chapter 7 – Work

5. **Always welcome inspection**

Don't get offended if the boss says, "I'd like to see that presentation," or "how are you making out on that project?" Welcome inspection. Your attitude should be "Sure, when do you want to come and take a look? I'd love to show you what I've done so far." This kind of attitude inspires confidence. Don't take on the attitude of "I thought you gave me this job because you thought I could do it. Don't you trust me?" This kind of attitude makes it seem as though you have something to hide. If you are open to inspection not only, can you showcase your efforts but you can benefit from the experience of your boss. Bosses will help you avoid pitfalls. Benefit from the wisdom of others, in the end, you will be more successful.

6. **Do more than what is expected**

Go above and beyond what is expected of you. People notice because it is so rare. Be the person who comes up with solutions. Don't dump problems on your boss's lap. He or she already has enough to deal with. If you bring up an issue, offer up a solution. This will be deeply appreciated. When you do your job with excellence without any hidden agendas, it won't be long before you move up. Do an honest day's work for an honest day's pay.

Why?

If you don't think you are getting paid enough, having a bad attitude won't get you more money. Having the right attitude will open up the door to promotion and to all the advantages that it brings.

7. **Move On**

Sometimes you just have to move on to take the next step. I'm not suggesting that you move every year from one thing to the next. Give it a worthy try. Evaluate where you are every three, five, and ten years. If it's working for you, continue; if not explore your options. Take a breather to think. Sometimes getting away from something for a short period of time can help give you clarity as to what your next step should be.

8. **Go for it**

Be Bold. Go after what you want. Don't be wishy-washy. You have to have a "go for it or die attitude." When you do, you will know that you gave it your best and you won't live with regrets.

9. **Be Consistent**

Consistency is the key to breakthrough. If you are not consistent and persistent, success will be elusive. This principle is extremely important. You can have many qualities but if you lack this one you can hit your head against the wall, asking yourself, "Why am I stuck?"

10. **Celebrate**

Whatever you do, don't ever make the mistake of not celebrating your successes. Sometimes we can get into a rut. Sometimes we get so busy with doing that we don't take out the time just to be and to enjoy. You have to have balance. How would you feel if you didn't take the time to recharge? What if you didn't take the time to do the things that you love? How would you feel if you lived in isolation, only focused on work and never taking the time to be with the people you love? What if life became a chore instead of an adventure? What if you felt like your well of creativity had run dry? Don't spend so much time focused on the hard work that you don't take the time to just live and have fun. Don't be like a car that runs out of fuel and is running on fumes. Take the time to celebrate you. Take the time to feel alive. Find things that energize you and live life all out because the alternative just plain sucks.

Why?

Life Killers:

Apathy

I heard a quote that is attributed to Albert Einstein. It says:

> **"There are only two ways to live your life. One is as though nothing is a miracle. The other is a though everything is a miracle."**

Apathy is defined as lack of interest, enthusiasm, or concern. Apathy is when you simply do not have any interest in moving forward, no motivation. Life just passes you by and you remain frozen. You are running on a low frequency. That is not the way to win the day. That is not the way to win life. So how do you turn that around? By definition empathy is the opposite of apathy. Without empathy or compassion, you cannot move into action. Without empathy it is difficult to be passionate about anything. When you open your heart, when you allow yourself to feel. When you stop being shut down, then you can start taking action. When you take action, you can start sharing the unique gifts you have. As you share the best of yourself, everyone benefits. Don't allow apathy to keep you from your destiny and reward.

Passivity

Passivity is acceptance of what happens, without active response or resistance. Passivity is the mindset of accepting just enough instead of more than enough. It's accepting the ordinary instead of the extraordinary. Passivity unplugs you from living. It cuts off all your chances at having a fulfilling life. Passivity says that things are always going to be the same and they are never going to change so why resist. Passivity is a life devoid of potential. Passivity tells you it's okay to conform, to go with the crowd instead of doing what is right for you. Passivity tells you that it is okay to do nothing because you can't expect any better. Doing nothing is the quickest path to going nowhere. Being content says I'm at peace with myself, life, and others. They are not the same and should not be confused.

Why?

Mom's Advice:	Work to earn a living, but don't forget to live.
Key Point:	Pursue excellence in your work. Be consistent.
Guiding Principle:	"Whatever you do [whatever your task may be], work from the soul [that is, put in your very best effort], as [something done] for the Lord and not for men." (Colossians 3:23 AMP)
Recommended Resources:	**On Entrepreneurship:** *The 4-hour work week* by Timothy Ferriss **On Work:** *The Principles* by Ray Dalio
Recommended Program:	**On productivity:** *Insane Productivity* by Darren Hardy www.darenhardy.com

Notes:

Chapter Eight

Money

Question: How do I manage my money?

What is in it for me? Freedom.

Why am I telling you this? I want you to live a great life. Money is a tool. Depending on how you use money, it can either be good or bad. Money makes a great servant but a lousy master. It can give you wings or tie you down in chains. Choose wisely.

The Back Story

When Gabrielle got married, she had no debt whatsoever. She didn't own anything, but she didn't owe anything either. This was a good position to start off a marriage. To Gabrielle money was important to have, but it wasn't something that consumed her. Her husband Scott, on the other hand worshiped money. He loved money because of what it could give him. Money meant that he was important, that he measured up.

Why?

He was always chasing after the almighty dollar. It was his god. She wondered why he went after it so hard. The only conclusion she could come up with was that he did it because having money defined him. It made him feel like a man. When he had money in his pocket he felt like a worthwhile human being. Gabrielle thought it was tragic that he only felt good when he had money in his pocket. She asked him, "What happens when you lose your job or the money dries up?" He answered, "You just go out and find a way to make more money." She thought, that was just a Band-Aid. You can cover up the problem but the problem is still there. It's understandable, men feel good when they are out making cash. Gabrielle applauded him for going out there every day and giving it all he had. The problem was that he thought he needed more money to be enough and he was already more than enough. He was smart, personable, hardworking, generous and funny. But it was as if he was blind to all his other qualities. It's as if he dismissed them and only thought of himself as an ATM machine. He convinced himself that no one would want him if he had no money, including his wife and children. He sabotaged their marriage. He would say she didn't need him because she was an independent woman. He felt like there was

Chapter 8 – Money

no reason for him to be in the marriage if he wasn't the provider. Unfortunately, he missed the part about being the leader of his home and guiding his family. The part about being the protector of the family and so many other things that define a man rather than just a paycheck. He changed jobs a lot, always looking for the next big thing that would pay him more. Instead of taking the time to build something that is lasting, he jumped from one thing to the next. The more he chased after money, the more it ran away from him. At one point he ended up with no job, selling everything he had, and living in his car. And it wasn't because he was looking for adventure or doing some soul-searching. He could've made better choices that wouldn't have led him there but he thought he needed the money. It was tragic because he had the potential to do and be anything he wanted to be. He could've rocked the world. He was amazing and just didn't see who he really was because he saw himself in only one way.

I don't know if the reason for his distorted view was that he needed validation. He had a terrible relationship with his father. They had nothing in common. His father humiliated him on a regular basis and never validated him in any way. Because he was a sensitive child, he needed more support. It's as if he

Why?

never healed from his childhood. He is still chasing money and continually struggling. It's important for each and every one of us to know that we have more value than a paycheck. Know that you are worth so much more.

Money

Money can help you live the life of your dreams, help change the lives of others, or give you power. Chasing money may take you places you may not want to go. How you use it reflects what's in your heart. Develop a healthy relationship with it so you can live a good life. Money gives you choices.

Make sure you have balance in your relationship with money. Money at its best is useful and necessary. Money at its worse is a terrible jailer. If you become obsessed with money, it will rule your life and you will be the one that suffers the pain of letting it run your life. Don't draw your self-worth from money. This is a trap. Will there ever be enough money to fill the void? Only God can fill that hole. Once you have the money, will you obsess over the possibility of losing it all and in the process lose yourself?

Debt

Don't get into debt. Debt is slavery. Debt is your worst enemy.

Chapter 8 – Money

It is the enemy to your financial future: don't entertain it. Pay cash. Debt will keep you strapped. Don't fall into the buy now, pay later trap. Save up for stuff that you want; I know it's old fashioned, but it will keep you stable. Have good debt, not bad debt. What do I mean? Let's say you get a loan for the purpose of a financial investment that will not only yield the payback of the loan but also a profit for you this kind of debt is o.k. to have temporarily. Getting a credit card with a ridiculously high interest rate to buy stuff you can't wait to have and then making the minimum payment is an example of bad debt. Be wise and only act if you have peace. There's a fine line: be very careful with money. If you don't control it, it's like a runaway train. Save it. Invest it. Give your money a goal and a purpose. Make your money work for you. Set your mind for success when it comes to money.

Love of Money

Many people think that money fixes everything. Some people think that "money is the root of all evil," but that's not quite right. The Bible says "the love of money is the root of all evil." It is having lustful relationship with money that is the root of all evil. Be balanced. Yes, it is the man's pride and joy to provide for

Why?

his family. However, do not get so obsessed with money that you forget about everything else. Ask yourself: why am I pursuing this money? Every time you do something, ask yourself why you are doing it. Is it to make you feel more important? Is it to fill some emptiness? Is it because you like the rush and the challenge?

> "For what will it profit a man if he gains the whole world [wealth, fame, success], but forfeits his soul?"
> (Matthew 16:26 AMP)

Money, at its best should be available to provide you a comfortable life and to have some left over to make a positive difference in the lives of others. Look at any men who are philanthropists, that's exactly what they do. Pitbull is known as a musician. Yes, he makes a lot of money as Mr. Worldwide but there is much more. He does philanthropic work that helps children, families and youth. In the end, there is just so much money you need.

You must be the master of your money, not the other way around. When money rules you, it is a tyrant. It tells you what to do and how to do it. Usually, it convinces you that it will be gratifying but ultimately it ruins you. Money will convince you

Chapter 8 – Money

that spending it on recreational drugs is just a good time - until you end up in rehab. Money will convince you that you can have any woman you want and that you will be the man…until you get a disease. Money will disguise itself as good and only lead you down a path of destruction.

Your attitude about Money

We have talked about some of the negative pitfalls of money. Now let's talk about the possibilities of money. It was amazing to me to discover that we develop a mindset about money. And just like many of our core values, our mindset can come from our parents, friends, authority figures, teachers, the media, our culture, etc. In T. Harv Eker's *Secrets of the Millionaire Mind* he explores what he calls "your money blueprint." He talks about having your thermostat set. You can have it set for success or failure. It discusses the psychology of wealth and success. It tells you what it takes to set your mind for success and keep it there. Many of us don't even realize we have inherited a blueprint for failure. It is not until you examine this area of your life that you realize where you stand. Eker's book talks about the mindset of rich people versus poor people. One that sticks out in my mid specifically is that rich people focus on opportunity while poor

Why?

people focus on the obstacles. Eker's book gives 17 ways that rich people think and act differently from poor people. It speaks to the attitudes that either empower you or disempower you when it comes to money. There are countless books out there that talk about money, how to manage it and how to invest it. I have listed a few at the end of this chapter. The difference in Eker's book is that it focuses on your mindset for money. It talks about the reasons, the psychology behind why you have or don't have money. Are you stuck in a cycle of self-sabotage? Can you break from this vicious cycle? The answer is yes. You can be free from a poor money blueprint. First you must recognize that it's that it exists and then you can start taking the steps to rid yourself of it.

Money with a mission

We all talk about money and how it affects our lives. Money is certainly a key player but it should never be our god. Money is a tool. Learn to use it effectively and wisely. Start with the basics. Always make sure to set aside 10% for helping others, charity, or giving. Always make sure to pay yourself at least 10%, this is your savings. Pay yourself as much as you give away. Set aside 10% for investing and creating passive income streams. Make your money work for you. This money is never spent it is only invested. 10% should go into an education fund for anything that will help edify you and give you additional skills and knowledge. Set aside 10% in a play account this is the one you use to have fun. Why? So that you can enjoy the fruits of your hard work, do something that will make you feel great. The other 50% is for necessities, paying bills and so forth. Setting up your finances like this essentially puts you in control instead of money controlling you. You get to enjoy it along the way while you are building a future for yourself. The sooner you start working with money this way, the sooner it will become second nature. Start saving and investing at an early age – don't wait! Why should you?

10%	Help Others
10%	Save
10%	Invest
10%	Continuing Education / Personal Development
10%	Fun / reward yourself
50%	Bills / necessities

Why?

Ok, so I know you are probably sitting there thinking "Are you nuts, who does that?" Who can actually live on half of what they make? Perhaps it can look like this, one month you take 10% and put it into your savings fund. Another month into your fun or investing fund. Get the idea? It's something that you can gradually work towards. This is something to aspire to.

There are examples of young people taking strong leadership roles and becoming millionaires by the time they are of legal age and some billionaires before they are 30. I encourage you to search it online since any example I could give you here would be outdated by the time this book is published. I will say that Farrah Gray who is now an international best-selling author, and motivational speaker stood out to me. He is known for being one of the youngest self-made millionaires owning a wealth of 1.5 million dollars by the time he was 14. He was also the youngest person to have a Wall Street office. He began his entrepreneurial journey when he was 6 selling lotions in his neighborhood. The moral of the story is start early. Build your wealth. Some might say "isn't that materialistic?" Not at all. The goal of money, at least in God's economy, is for the purpose of helping others. If someone has a dire need sometimes the answer to a prayer is money. Let's be practical: if someone is about to lose their house in a foreclosure, what that person needs, is money. Here is your opportunity to be an asset and not a liability.

Why should you be an asset to someone? On a practical note, the tax break helps lower your taxable income when you file your taxes. My hope is that you would want to invest in others for unselfish reasons. There is the saying, "What goes around comes around." You get out of something what you put into it. In God's way of doing things, He rewards us for taking care of each other. You may not need to be rewarded with money, but what if you needed health or a good marriage? The good you do for others, God will do for you. Think about Christmas time and how great it makes you feel to give someone something they really wanted. You cannot put a price on seeing someone happy or knowing your life here on this earth is making a difference. The joy and the peace in your heart are good reasons too.

Practical tips to manage your money
Track where you are spending your money; that will tell you very quickly where your priorities are. It will also tell you where you can cut back so that you can put more money in your pocket.

Why?

1. Make a budget & follow it.

    a. Dave Ramsey's Financial Peace University is a great place to start no matter what stage of life you are in.

2. Track where your money is going.

    a. A simple spreadsheet works.

    b. Some banks include budget trackers as part of their online banking; use it.

    c. Good Budget is a good app for beginners and has a free version (at the time of this book's publication).

3. Pay cash.

4. Stay out of debt.

    a. Get rid of credit card debt.

    b. Some folks ascribe to the use of credit cards being o.k. as long as you pay them monthly because they have lucrative rewards programs. That can work as long as you keep some kind of fund to cover what you put on the card. But it's like playing with fire you might get burned unless you are careful.

    c. Get rid of student loans.

        i. Fill out the FAFSA to get federal aid.

Chapter 8 – Money

      ii. Try getting scholarships or grants instead of incurring the loan debt.

      iii. Use pre-paid college plans and 529 college savings plans wherever possible.

      iv. If you do have loans, try re-financing at lower rates.

  d. Get rid of car loans.

      i. By the way, it is best not to lease a vehicle unless it is part of a business right off and you have a legitimate plan for leasing.

5. Find $ in your current situation.

  a. What can you sell?

  b. Can you save with coupons or Groupon?

  c. Can you barter?

  d. Can you buy used or refurbished?

  e. Can you consign or thrift?

  f. What are you spending too much money on?

      i. Eating out.

      ii. Entertainment.

      iii. Coffee.

Why?

       iv. Sports equipment.

       v. Clothes.

       vi. Furnishings.

6. Keep an emergency fund of $1,000-3,000.

7. Save 6-12 months of salary. If you lose your job, you are covered and don't need to panic. You can take your time to find the job you want versus taking the one you need.

8. Invest. Make your money go to work for you.

In the previous chapter I talked about types of work and I mentioned investing. If you are young and just getting started in the world, don't just think "job." Get the job, but make the most of it. Think of how the job can contribute to your investment. First, get the experience. Take advantage of any and all training and certification programs. These are very valuable and you don't have to pay for them. If they offer rotational programs, mentorships or shadowing get involved in those. This is where you learn while getting paid. Don't underestimate what a good deal this is for you. Leverage the company resources as much as possible. Invest in yourself.

Chapter 8 – Money

When you start work look for companies who contribute to your finances. I don't mean just the paycheck. Beyond the training programs I mentioned before, companies often offer a savings program such as a 401K. In some places, for every dollar you put in, the company puts in a dollar. Two for one, yay! This is money you can invest.

Use the company's 401K and max it out, especially if the company is matching funds. Open a cash account with a brokerage. Use that account to start putting money away. You will get better interest than in the bank. Once you have built it up a bit, use some of the money to invest in other places. Don't just trade the time for money and then not put the money to work. You are never too young to start. Time goes by very quickly and before you know it you can find yourself nearing your 60's in debt and having no savings. That is no way to live. The sooner you become financially independent, the more you can enjoy your life and live the destiny you were created for.

Own, do not rent

If at all possible, own your home do not rent. I grew up in New York and with prices being what they are, I never thought it was an option. Start off small. Buy a small co-op or condo in another state to start. Let it gain some equity. Plan for your next purchase. Move up little by little. Don't bite off more than you can chew. It is not worth the stress. It will have you over-committed and it will deny you the extra money you can have to enjoy where you are while you are planning for where you are going. Owning gives you the potential for equity; renting does not. Buy when prices are low and wait until prices get high to sell. You can take that appreciation and use it for your next wealth building step.

Get a financial advisor

First thing is first: don't get an advisor who is just a sales guy pushing financial products. These kinds of advisors are a "dime a dozen." Get an advisor, preferably one that is certified and has many years of experience. One who is focused on helping you achieve your goals and doesn't have a conflict of interest. I would look for an advisor who is not tied to any specific brokerage house and who only makes money if he or she makes your portfolio grow. Credit unions offer advisors and often they are not tied to any brokerage house. What that means for you is that you get more options for your portfolio. Make sure that in this relationship you keep each other accountable. Get started early, as soon as you hit the workforce. But what do I need an advisor for if I don't have any money? Start from where you are. The best advice I can give is to hold on to your money and stay out of debt. Even if you put $25 away every time you get paid, you would be amazed how much money you would have in a year. Once you've done all of those it is time to plan. Set up your goals. If you had all the money you needed at your disposal, what things would you do? Put these goals on paper, put absolute deadlines as to when you will achieve these goals. Place dollar amounts beside them, decide what you are getting out of having these goals and if they don't line up with your values, get rid of them. You have to make sure you want to invest your time and or money to whatever goal you have set. In Kenneth Himmler's book *Live Rich Stay Wealthy* he goes into detail about the types of goals you can set. These can include things like paying off debt, educating children, purchasing a home, or vacations for example.

Money in God's system

There is no way to cover the topic of money in a small chapter

Why?

like this. The little bit of information I have put in here doesn't even begin to cover the intricacy of money. I know that what I have presented here is overly simplistic. It is just a place to start with some basics. There are countless books about money from people that know a heck of a lot more about it than me. Read and learn. It will be worth your while.

Funny enough, I never considered that God might have something to say about money. In fact, you would be surprised to know that the Bible mentions money more than 800 times. I thought God was supposed to guide me on spiritual things, not on practical things. I was wrong.

I had gone through Dave Ramsey's Financial Peace University program and in fact I had taught the material in several small groups and in one very large group at church. It took a lot of discipline, but the program worked quite well for me. I was patting myself on the back. This program made sense to me because it was practical.

In my continued desire to learn more I ordered a package that was offered on TV by Faith Life Now ministries. There were some audio CD's and a book called *Money Mysteries from the Master* by Gary Keesee. I glanced the cover and thought "yeah right, that's going to be a lot of help, now let's just over-spiritualize money." I thought it was going to be yet another book that takes me down a rabbit trail only to tell me some basic stuff I already know. But I thought to myself, *I'll give it a chance, what can it hurt, I might learn something.*

In the book Keesee explains that God's way of dealing with money is different than the world's way of dealing with money. It is counterintuitive and it requires faith and trust. However, it is effective and not only duplicates but multiplies. It is overabundant because that's just the way God is. God's way with money has a few basic principles.

1. **Seed time and harvest time**

    You have to give it away to get it back with interest. This is the principle of seed time and harvest time. Which usually ends up more like seed…time…harvest. It is the time between the seed and the harvest where a lot of people miss their blessing because they become impatient.

2. **Strategy**

    God will give you a unique idea or strategy that will propel you forward. The treasure you seek is a gift that God has already planted on the inside of you.

3. **Timing**

   When you get an idea from God you need to act quickly. When you procrastinate the moment is gone and the opportunity along with it. Be swift. Take action immediately. Not doing so can be a very painful lesson.

4. **Preparation**

   You need to prepare. Each step you take brings you closer to the intended goal. No matter how hard the lesson. No matter how insignificant the next step may seem, push forward. You are being prepared for something great.

5. **Trust**

   This journey of financial freedom does not come without trusting God's divine plan. Trust that your financial freedom is tied to your destiny. If the enemy catches on to what God has for you expect some opposition. When it comes, continue going forward. Arriving at your destination will prompt people to ask "How did you do it?" Just the fact of arriving can speak volumes regarding God's goodness and the many blessings of following Him. The icing on the cake is the financial freedom that will allow you not only to do what you are destined to do, but to also occupy that territory. One key note here. The reason the enemy attacks your identity so hard is because he knows that if you are weak in this area he can cripple you. Why does he hit you here? Because he knows that your destiny, your success is tied to your healthy self-identity. When your identity is strong there is nothing, you can't accomplish or believe.

6. **Obedience**

   You may receive instructions that simply won't make any kind of sense. You will think that you are the least qualified person to do what God is asking you to do.

   Remember in your weakness He is strong. Obey. Follow the instructions even when it seems crazy. When you do you will come out on the other side as a champion.

7. **Patience**

   You may also be in training for a long time. Patience will be required. You will want to quit a million times. Never quit.

Partner up

When you are going to sow seed make sure you are sowing into good ground. What do I mean by that? If you are giving of your money and you are expecting a return on your seed make sure that the ministry you are partnering with believes as you do. What is the point of partnering? The blessing that is on the successful ministry will overflow to you because you are both in agreement. Do not sow to a ministry that is not in agreement with what you believe otherwise you will be throwing your money away.

8. **Profit**

When David beat Goliath, he didn't ask questions about Goliath he asked what will be done for the man who takes care of the problem. That is the question to ask. What is the gain? The key here is that David took care of God's business and then God took care of David. When you look at what you can do for God, which ultimately is tied to helping people, then you can see great profit in your investment.

9. **Give only in faith**

STOP! THIS IS IMPORTANT!

Give only in faith. Many people give out of duty, because they think that's what they are supposed to do. Others give because that's what traditional religion has taught them. Some give because they have been manipulated to give. Still others do it because they treat it like a formula. If I give then that means that God will give me X back. "The power of God's anointing flows through faith and not formula."*

Again, I have oversimplified here. To really grasp these concepts, I recommend that you read the book. If you want to put God's supernatural blessings on your natural abilities learning these concepts will give you a new perspective that can radically change your life. It is a crucial read.

Life Builders:

1. **Use money as a tool.** Learn as much as you can about how to use money as a tool.

2. **Know where your money is going.** If you don't know where it's going, it will go everywhere and not where you want it to go. Don't spend it all.

* Keese, Gary. "The Power of Faith." *Money Mysteries from the Master*, Destiny Image Publishers, 2011, p.180

Why?

3. **Give your money a mission.** Create a budget and stick to it. Create an emergency fund.

4. **Save.** Start when you are young. If you save you will always have money when you need it. Compound interest and residual income are your best friends.

5. **Make your money work for you.** Invest it. Find sources of residual income. Learn as much as you possibly can about how to create and retain wealth. The bigger problem that you solve the more money you will have.

6. **Have Fun**

Life Killers:

1. **Don't let money control you.** Money serves you. You don't serve money.

2. **Debt. Stay out of it.** You are a slave to whomever you owe money to.

3. **Don't let poor use of money ruin your life.** Indulging in all your desires can hurt you. Is it a want or a need?

4. **Envy.**

Stay in your lane. Your journey is yours only. Don't compare. Don't look horizontally only look vertically. What am I saying?

Look up. Look only to where you are going. Never mind what anyone else is doing. That's their life not yours. You are only responsible for your own life. The minute you compare, you wish you had what someone else has you have lost your focus. It is their time, not your time. Your time will come too. Envying what someone else has is a sure way to be miserable. Find the way to make your mark in the world. The bigger problem you solve the more money that comes with it. Don't serve yourself; serve others. Not only will you reap a financial reward but you will also have the joy of having made this world a better place for everyone.

Why?

Mom's Advice:	Manage your money, save, invest, avoid debt, and be generous…give.
Key Point:	Money is a tool. Use it for good. Send it to do what you want. Grow it and invest it.
Guiding Principle:	"But if it's only money these leaders are after, they'll self-destruct in no time. Lust for money brings trouble and nothing but trouble. Going down that path, some lose their footing in the faith completely and live to regret it bitterly ever after." (1 Timothy 6:10 MSG)
Recommended Resources:	**On money:** *Rich Dad, Poor Dad* by Robert Kiyosaki **On money:** *Money, Master the Game: 7 Simple Steps to Financial Freedom* by Tony Robbins **On money:** *Live Rich, Stay Wealthy* by Kenneth Himmler, Sr. **On money:** *Money Mysteries from the Master* by Gary Keesee (This is a crucial read)
Recommended Programs	**On money:** *Financial Peace University* by Dave Ramsey **On money:** *Debt Free Degree* by Dave Ramsey

Notes:

CHAPTER NINE

Time

Question: How do I spend my time?

What is in it for me? Time well spent is a life well lived.

Why am I telling you this?

Time is the one thing that you can never get back, or make more of. Once you spend the time it is over. Make sure that the way you spend your time lines up with the priorities for your life. Giving your time to things that are not important to you, is giving your life away. If your priorities have a lasting impact, then your life will have a lasting impact too.

The Back Story

I worked for a very successful man when I was transitioning from my TV career to my recruiting career. He was successful despite himself. He was intelligent, focused and resilient. He was also disorganized, lacked integrity in some areas, and did not listen to anyone. Oh, and yes, he was a drunk. In spite of it,

Why?

I think deep down he was good hearted. No one is ever all good or all bad. Here was a man that could have been very successful. Sure, he lived in a big house and drove a nice car but he was so far in debt that he was one bad move from being destitute. He had a beautiful wife and wonderful children. They even had a nanny brought exclusively from Europe to take care of the kids. He was someone who was larger than life and I liked that about him. There was never a dull moment when he was around. However, he carried a deep gaping hole in his heart. A very dear friend of his was killed in a shooting. I don't think he ever recovered from it. In fact, he named his first-born son after his friend. The tragedy is that he carried that pain with him for a very long time. It changed his life in a very dramatic way. He struggled with the pain and looked for satisfaction in external things that never filled that hole. It is a tragedy to see young men with good hearts end up as men with broken, hardened hearts. I guess he figured "What does it all mean anyway?" One minute your life is going in one direction and a minute later everything has changed. I guess he just decided to dull the pain with temporary pleasures just living the moment. The sad thing is that he missed out on the amazing people he already had in

Chapter 9 – Time

his life. He had a wife who loved him and children that needed him. He was partial to the oldest son and his second son really didn't get much of his attention. How different his life could have been if he decided to deal with the pain in healthier ways. How different his life could have been had he applied the same discipline and relentless pursuit in building a life for himself as he had done in building his business. When you are given a life worth living don't waste it on regrets. Don't get me wrong, I am not belittling the memory of his dear friend, nor minimizing the agonizing pain he must have felt. What I am saying is don't lose sight of the good things in your life. Don't waste your life on fleeting pleasures that disappear but rather spend your time on things that last like a loving family. Spend your time on things that add value to both your life and to others.

Time

Don't waste time. This is your most precious commodity. You can always make more money but you can't make more time. The activities you choose are what you trade in for your time; choose wisely. A minute gone is a minute you will never get back. Don't waste your time on self-pity, anger hatred, self-loathing, and revenge. For that matter don't waste your time on procrastination or laziness either. None of these things yield any kind of fruit. All of these are devices for your destruction. Spend your time loving, laughing, learning, giving, these things bear fruit that are lasting and enhance the quality of your life. A doctor I know went to Princeton and then pursued her medical degree at Tufts University. At the time, I'm sure she could've chosen the library or a party. I know she chose the library many more times than a party. Today she has a very successful practice. In fact, she is a pediatric specialist. Her choices made yesterday are making a difference in the lives of many children today. She chose wisely and it has yielded fruit not only for her but for the lives of others.

The way you choose how to spend your time today can impact future generations. Famous examples are people like Henry Ford, Thomas Edison, and Walt Disney. The way these men chose to spend their time has impacted countless of lives but also left a future for the generations in their family. What can seem like an insignificant choice at the time can really make all the difference in the world. This is not to put pressure to be perfect all the time but just a word to let you know that even though it may be hard sometimes to make the more excellent choice, in the end it will be worth it.

I met a young woman who had an alcoholic mother and a father that was addicted to drugs. At 16 she got pregnant. The amazing thing about her is that her story was not shaping up the way we might all expect. It was miraculous and different. At the time when she had her first baby she was living with some friends and found out that they were selling drugs in the apartment. The mere idea that her child might be taken from her because of what was going on around her was so repulsive that she went out and got her own place to live. She got a job and she chose to fight for her family. The child's father also stepped up and decided to take care of his son. Together they unselfishly put the needs of their children before their own. My point in telling you this is that even when under dire circumstances, you can always make the more excellent choice. You can choose to spend your time in a way that makes a difference not only in your life but in the lives of others. If you learn from the past, you can live your best life today and leave a legacy for tomorrow.

Practical use of your time
Live intentionally. Spend your time on the things that are of

Why?

value. Spend your time on the things that support your value system and goals. When you are trying to focus on passing an important exam for school or when you are trying to finish up that very important business plan; a small thing like a ringing phone can be a devastating distraction. That phone will suck up your time with something that is not going to get you closer to your goal. You will constantly have these things come at you and you must stay focused. When I was getting started in my career the company, I worked for had us take a Franklin Covey Time Management Seminar. I thought back then, what a waste. I don't need anyone to tell me how to manage my time. I am a very organized person, I always have a check list of what needs to get done, what do I need this for? As with many things, I later realized that I should've been open to learning. Later on, when I was no longer a single career woman but a wife, a mother, a business manager, and an aspiring writer, I realized that I needed to make better use of my time. I had to analyze my value system; I had to think about my mission statement in the various areas of my life. And mostly I had to manage my time. I hope that you are not as naïve and hard headed as me. I recommend that you either read or listen to Stephen Covey's

Chapter 9 – Time

audio book *The 7 Habits of Highly Effective People*. If you can avoid the pitfalls, please do.

Getting started early in life with a clear vision of your goals for your personal life, career, finances, spiritual growth, and legacy will make your walk far less frustrating. It will yield a more satisfying life and get you ahead of the game. God says that there are only two things that are eternal; His word and people. Guide your priorities by things that are eternal. Do not squander your time!

Having fun

You have a right to a happy life. Life is not complete without fun. Having a successful life involves being complete, whole, nothing missing lacking or broken in your life. It is difficult to get there without taking time to re-energize yourself. Don't become such a workaholic that you don't take time for you and for the people that matter to you. I know as a mom I have struggled with taking time for me. I have learned that if I don't take the time to relax every once in a while, that I become stale and angry. No one can benefit from me if my life is out of balance. Having balance is really important. There is a time for everything in life. The Bible says that there is a time to laugh and a time to cry. You shouldn't get stuck in either one for too long. Having a good time is important to your health and sanity; just make sure it doesn't become your obsession. Some people use it to hide from pain or responsibilities. Sometimes people use it as a way to avoid growing and maturing. Hiding in having a good time has a high price; usually it's wasted time and the loss of vision for your life. Being mature gives you strength for living. It gives you what you need to live a thriving life. Travel, do sports, stay with friends, lie on the beach, do an extreme sport, go to events, try something different; the important thing is to be open to life and to living. Be careful not to make your world too small.

Balance

Balance, what a small word and what a big challenge it can present. Balance requires making wise choices. The challenge is that sometimes we can't tell what a wise choice is. My best advice is not to get into extremes. Extremes have a way of getting us out of balance in a hurry. Every choice will either propel you further ahead or hinder you. As you think about how to balance work, relationships, play or anything else, think before acting. Don't make rash decisions. Ask yourself; "How does this decision impact the direction of my life and that of my family?" If your decision opens new possibilities versus hindrances, it is probably a good choice.

Life Builders:

Build margin into your life. Here are some tips that I think can help.

1. Arrive everywhere 15 minutes earlier than you have to be there it will help you go through your day without stress.

2. Focus on one major project at a time. Trying to do too many things at once makes things hard to manage and nothing gets accomplished.

3. Stay in the important not urgent quadrant. Franklin Covey's Time Matrix is a time management tool that helps individuals prioritize tasks based on their urgency and importance. Divided into four quadrants, the matrix allows users to classify activities to focus on what truly adds value, avoiding distractions and the overload of urgent but non-essential tasks. By applying this method, one can improve productivity, reduce stress, and dedicate more time to strategic goals and personal growth.

4. Find time to decompress.

Why?

	URGENT	**NOT URGENT**
IMPORTANT	**Q1 NECESSITY** Crises Emergency meetings Last-minute deadlines Pressing problems Unforeseen events	**Q2 EFFECTIVENESS** Proactive work Important goals Creative thinking Planning and prevention Relationship building Learning and renewal Recreation
NOT IMPORTANT	**Q3 DISTRACTION** Needless interruptions Unnecessary reports Irrelevant meetings Other people's minor issues Unimportant email, tasks, phone calls, status posts, etc.	**Q4 WASTE** Trivial work Avoidance activities Excessive relaxation, television, gaming, Internet Time-wasters Gossip

Covey, Stephen. Franklin Covey. 2024, https://www.franklincovey.com/the-7-habits/habit-3/. Accessed 14 May 2024

Life Killers:

1. **Being late** - You will miss opportunities when you are late.

2. **Overcommitting** – Don't take on more than what you can handle.

3. **Going down the wrong track** – Make sure you are leading a life of significance.

4. **Wasting time** – Don't waste your time on things that don't matter.

Chapter 9 – Time

Mom's Advice:	Don't waste time. You will never get back lost time. Live with intention, with your goals in mind. Make sure you use your time wisely to build the satisfying, significant life that you dream of.
Key Point:	Time is precious, use it wisely.
Guiding Principle:	"For everything there is a season, and a time for every matter under heaven: a time to break down, and a time to build up; a time to weep, and a time to laugh; a time to mourn, and a time to dance." (Ecclesiastes 3:1, 3-4 NIV)
Recommended Resources:	**On Time Management:** *The 7 Habits of Highly Effective People* by Steven Covey **On Self-management:** *Eat That Frog!: 21 Great Ways to Stop Procrastinating and Get More Done in Less Time* by Brian Tracy

Why?

Notes:

Chapter Ten

God

Question: Why God?

What is in it for me? Connecting to the most powerful source in the universe will give you wings to fly.

Why am I telling you this?

I want the best for you. As a mother I wish I could be here for you always. I know however, that my time on earth is limited. The only person I know you can entrust your life to is God. I know Him to be loving and kind. I know he will look out for your best interest. He is always there even when you turn your back on him. He waits for you with the loving arms of a father ready to hug you and welcome you, home. Ready to spoil you and give you the best. Ready to listen to you. He has been my friend, my father, my protector, my provider, my guide and so much more.

Why?

I know that if you open your heart to Him he can be exactly what you need.

The Back Story

My first memory of God in my life was when I was around 5 years old. I lived in Puerto Rico in a simple wooden house with a zinc roof. I remember in the evenings my mom would have me kneel in the bedroom and together we would pray. I don't remember any of the prayers. I just remember that moment because it taught me that there was someone bigger than me that I could go to if I needed help. The most beautiful memory I have of God was when I went to Sunday school as a kid. You might think we met in a church building but we didn't. We sat in a lady's backyard. Her house was on top of a hill. Each of the kids sat somewhere on the ground and a lady spoke to us about God. Later she would give us crackers and hot chocolate. I think that was probably my favorite part. The reason I think I remember that so clearly is because I felt pure joy and peace. I remember it was a beautiful sunny day and we all enjoyed playing and laughing together. I think that's exactly the way God always wants to see his children: simply happy. It is said that God is love. Love in action is most definitely a reflection

Chapter 10 – God

of God's love. Because my mom took the time to teach me to pray and because our neighbor invested in us kids, that is why I still look to God today. Later on, we moved from Puerto Rico to New York. We started going to a Catholic Church. I remember sitting in a poufy dress with tights and black patent leather shoes falling asleep in an uncomfortable wooden pew. I spent many years sitting there and never got to know God any better. I had some concept of God but I never knew him. I remember being in church one day and praying to God saying, "Please tell me that this isn't all you are just a bunch of rituals and then leaving church feeling as empty as when I walked in the door." Little did I know that God would fulfill a promise in the Bible that says:

> "If you need wisdom, ask God for it. He will give it to you. God gives freely to everyone. He doesn't find fault."
> (James 1:5 NLV)

It took three years and the journey was not meant to discourage me but to strengthen me. I never have to wonder if God is paying attention or leading me down the right path. I eventually moved from New York to Atlanta and it was at World Changers Church International where I watarted to get some answers. Pastor Dollar

Why?

taught exactly what is in God's heart. Whether you believe me or not, that is exactly what the Bible is: a written documentation of God's heart for humanity. When I started to learn about God and really got to know Him, it was revolutionary. The idea that he was active and alive rocked my world. It amazes me when I think that it started with just a simple question "Show me where you are," and I finally found him in such an odd way, after a conversation in a parking lot with someone I knew. Keep your eyes open; you never know how and through whom he'll choose to make himself known to you. I am still inspired today by the way God kept his word to me and so grateful for that faithful person who had the courage to speak to me about God without being embarrassed, had he not done it, I might still be looking or worse have given up on finding Him. One thing you should remember above all else is that you need to get an understanding of God's love for you. Everything else will fall into place and make sense when you really understand His love. Be assured that just as I'm saying this to you that there will be scoffers: other people, various media, or some other sources that will claim that what I'm saying is just a crock. Please remember that this is normal and just another stumbling block on your

Chapter 10 – God

road to finding God. Don't think that once you decide to look for God that you're going to have a red-carpet experience. That's why I'm encouraging you never to give up. And not to sound too New Age or off the wall (maybe you already think I do), but God is everywhere. You have to open yourself to the Creator and his creation. The awesome power of God can be found as you look at the world around you; as you look at nature and at the balance of the universe. Looking at it from a scientific point of view, just consider your own human body and how science doesn't understand how it all works. Why are there still so many unanswered questions? Because God is God and we can't try to make ourselves into Him. We can't try to make sense of it all without Him. I know, I've tried it many times but it hasn't worked. I've just spent a lot of energy and have been very frustrated. And even as you walk with God, realize that not all your questions will be answered. God doesn't ever reveal his entire plan to you all at once.

He takes you one step at a time, but

> "The Law of the Lord is perfect, giving new strength
> to the soul. The Law He has made known is sure,
> making the child-like wise.

Why?

> "The Laws of the Lord are right, giving joy to the heart. The Word of the Lord is pure, giving light to the eyes."
> (Psalm 19:7-8 NLV)

There are things that have happened in my life that later on I was able to see why God allowed them to happen the way they did. The perfect example for me was my biological father. He wasn't around, he walked away when I was very young and never made any effort to get to know me. In fact, the only reason I even knew about him was because my mom would send me to Puerto Rico and arrange for me to meet him. I always wondered why he didn't seem to care. I always thought that his other kids had it better than me because he lived under the same roof with them. I later realized that I was the lucky one because I had a great stepdad who was there for me. All my life the only constant male figure has been my stepdad. I thought, *what is the point of having a father that is physically there but emotionally absent?* That is what my brothers and sisters experienced. Somehow, we always think we are getting cheated and instead God is being loving and gracious. I don't take having my stepdad lightly because he could have been anywhere but he stayed with Mom and me.

Chapter 10 – God

When you are looking for God

God's love seems like a fantasy. For a lot of people, experiencing God's love is not even something that they expect. Many believe that there is a God but don't consider him to be a living God, active and engaged in every detail of their lives. Without a revelation of God's love for you, it is difficult to have faith. Until you get a deep conviction of God's love for you, until it is in every pore of your body it's hard to believe in God for anything. You may say to me; Well, that's real nice that you are telling me this, thanks for sharing, but how do I make it a reality for me? The first thing to do is to look for Him. Never give up on having a deep personal relationship with God.

Most people think the obvious place to find God is in a church. But as my grandmother used to say, "God will meet you wherever you are." This is not a fantasy but a reality. God can meet you in your loneliness, in your desperation, in your hopelessness, wherever you happen to be. He met me in a parking lot.

Relationship with God vs. Religion

God and religion are two different things. Like so many others things that have gotten twisted this is one of them. Religion

Why?

says follow the rules or you will be punished. God says follow me and I will show you a way full of life. Many people have had religion forced upon them. Unfortunately,

> *Religion says follow the rules or you will be punished. God says follow me and I will show you a way full of life*

instead of receiving a message of hope, most of us have been victims of the caveman version. Many of us can relate to the one family member who just wants to grab you by the hair, clobber you over the head with a Bible, and drag you to church. Well, woo hoo…boy was that fun!

Listen, I understand what that's like. The approach has been wrong even though the intention was right. Sometimes the enthusiasm about the great news of freedom has had a terrible delivery team. God, on the other hand, is not a caveman but a gentleman. He always approaches us with caring and truth. He is clear in his ways but he always allows us to make the choice. How should the message be delivered? Primarily it should be delivered by the way we live. We should really be what we claim to be. We should be the personification of love, patience, and understanding, and this is how it should be delivered. By showing love and not judgement. We should be willing to be available and go the distance because not everyone will be ready for God at the same time. So, if there is someone kicking themselves for not being ready, the answer should be as God says, for everything there is a time and a season. It is vitally important that you be in step with God and his timing.

A lot of people have been wounded, emotionally, physically or have been violated. In many cases, by people they were supposed to trust. And the question lingers, where was God when this was happening to me? This is what I discovered, that the enemy is opportunistic. He preys on one person's weakness and uses it to victimize others. Unfortunately, in many cases, the aggressor victimizes others as a consequence of having been subjected to neglect in their own life. Lack of nurturing from one person unleashes a chain effect of pain and tragedy. The enemy takes advantage of that and kicks you when you are down.

So, where's God? Here's the thing, he never messes with a person's free will, he can't. He never forces or imposes himself on anybody. But He is there always to pick up the pieces. And I know that may not be a good enough answer. I decided that it was better to have him in my corner than not at all. I also

Why?

decided that it was useless to be angry at the one person that could help me. I allowed God to come in my life and I have seen him heal my wounds, restore my faith, give me confidence, keep me in safety. So, it worked for me, right? What makes me so sure it will work for you? I know God's love and he doesn't play favorites.

God is hard to explain but if I could draw a comparison, I would say He is like sheet music. When I look at sheet music, I don't understand all the symbols and mess up on the notes. But to a trained musician all of it makes perfect sense. The musician hears the music in a completely different way than I would; he simply understands that language. When you start practicing the word of God it's like the symbols, keys and notes become clearer and there is a fresh revelation of what God wants to show you that eventually puts a new song in your heart.

Everyone's journey is unique and it is important that you make it your own. When you read this, it may not mean so much but in time as you experience all He has to offer, these experiences will be as individual as you are. If I say to you that God heals, it will be a completely different experience for you than it has been for me or for anyone else. I want you to have Him as an inheritance when I'm gone because he will never leave you. He will stand by you always.

Why should I trust God?

Loving God and trusting God are two separate things. There was a time when I knew that I loved God but I just didn't trust him. A lot of bad things happened to me when I was young. I was really angry with God. I asked God, "Where were you when I was suffering?" You will ask the same question too. We all do. I realized that it wasn't God that brought this or that tragedy on me. I realized that it was the enemy coming to "steal, kill, and destroy." (John 10:10 AMP) It was evil coming squash me like a bug, to take away my right to a peaceful life. Things that I saw as a loss, I later realized were actually God protecting me. It's tough to trust God if you don't know him. Even though I sat in church for over 30 years, I never knew him. When I became a born-again Christian, God gave me a new beginning. He wiped the slate clean and gave me fresh start. He came to live inside of me, to help me. It was my first step to knowing him and it was then that my eyes were opened to really see what God had done for me. God says:

Why?

> "For I know the plans that I have for you, plans to prosper you and not to harm you; plans to give you hope and a future."
> (Jeremiah 29:11 NIV)

Trust God with your destiny. Why should I do that? It is ultimately the best road to travel. How can I say that so confidently? Try the road without him and then try the road with him, you'll find that the road with him is far better despite any challenges you can face. I'm writing this to let you know that there are endless promises for your good that God has left behind. It is up to you to go on that expedition to find them. Where do you go? You go to the word of God, is it that simple? Yes. But here is the key; you have to get a revelation of God's love before you can ever make any of those promises your own. You have to know in your heart, not just your head that the promises are specifically for you. And the only way to get there is by studying God's love and by reminding yourself of all the times that he has been there for you. Only in this way can you have the confidence to trust Him. As you do, you will discover there are going to be obstacles along the way. But anything worth having requires some effort on your

> *Obstacles are designed to discourage you but they can also strengthen you.*

Chapter 10 – God

part. Ultimate freedom will have a price. Why the obstacles? The obstacles are designed to discourage you but they can also strengthen you.

> "These trials will show you that your faith is genuine. It is being tested as fire tests and purifies gold — though your faith is far more precious than mere gold. So when your faith remains strong through many trials, it will bring you much praise and glory and honor" (1 Peter 1:7 TLB)

We all want happiness and freedom. God offers you this and more. But do you think that the enemy (evil, forces of darkness, the devil) is just going to roll over and play dead. He's going to fight you. Why? Because he wants to convince you that there isn't a God; that this is just some fantasy. Again, I'm not talking about a bunch of rules and regulations. Religion is like a cruel taskmaster. In a relationship with Jesus there is freedom. He says because I am giving you my power and it lives inside of you, you'll only want to do good things. Things that not only bless you but make a difference for others. As you gain, others gain too. Don't kid yourself; you were born at this exact moment in time because you have been divinely given the ability to face all the challenges of this day and age. With that ability you can carve a destiny for yourself and impact the world. You can be an ambassador to Christ shinning the light of God inside of you giving people hope for a better present. Giving others the same kind of enthusiasm for living as you have.

Motivational speakers & coaches will teach you to get your mind off the problem and change your train of thought. This is exactly what God is talking about. Don't stay in the same thought patterns. Don't put yourself down. If you want to succeed at anything you have to change your way of thinking. Another teaching of motivational coaches is to start doing whatever it is you've been wanting to do. Do it, today, don't put it off. When you do those two things it is the beginning of your expedition to your destiny. When you really follow the desire of your heart and you are living that desire, you can't help but to feel fulfilled.

So why not just get some motivational audio files and just follow what the coaches say? Many of these coaches know personally what it's like to live a defeated life and turn it around. They can give some very good advice. The difference with God on your side is that you don't have to do it in your own power. You can overcome problems quicker with God's wisdom than with just your own. As you take the action to walk toward God He walks toward you. As you do your part, He will meet you where you are and help you in places where you are weak. It's a beautiful dance of following His lead, and putting your own personality into whatever you build together.

Don't judge God by what people do

People are flawed. People make mistakes. People sometimes will say and do things they later regret. How incredibly unfortunate to have to say this but sometimes Christians don't do things the way God would want them to. As a result, they give God a bad reputation. The very people who are supposed to show compassion and love and understanding are the first people to stand in judgement. That's why so many people don't want anything to do with Christians. I can't say that I blame them. I didn't want anything to do with them either. I didn't want to be like them. I told myself if I couldn't be the real deal I wanted no part of it. So many bad things have been done in the name of religion. I don't want religion. I want a close personal relationship with God.

Sometimes the price you have to pay is getting past those people who get in the way. I'm not saying to put up with people's nonsense I'm saying find a place where you can get to know him better. I have been very fortunate to have been part of churches that focused on God's word and welcoming everyone and I mean everyone. Don't expect perfection. Every time we have expectations people will disappoint us. That's a fact. The reason is that no one is perfect and people can't perform perfectly all the time. Don't allow anyone or anything get in the way of your relationship with God. There is so much that He wants to give you. Have you ever been driving down the road, gotten distracted by something and ended up in an accident? The enemy wants to get your eyes off God and distract you with the things that are around you until you crash and burn. When you do, the enemy disappears, he laughs at you and leaves you in your mess. But God, comes to heal you and to love you.

Does God really love me?

> "Your GOD is present among you, a strong Warrior there to save you. Happy to have your back, he'll calm you with his love and delight you with his songs."
> (Zephaniah 3:17 MSG)

When I first saw this Bible verse all I could say was "Wow".

Chapter 10 – God

"Why would anyone want to do that for me? Who loves that deeply?" Just for a minute I allowed myself to believe that maybe it could be true. What if He was the real deal? What if He really means what He says? It blew my mind. I started to think do I really know Him? Who is this God? What does He want from me? What would this relationship look like? In life, you rarely have anyone come to you willing to give you so much without wanting something from you. In the end, I discovered that all He wanted was me. Just to be with me. To talk to me. To be my friend. A very powerful friend who can do for me what no one else can.

One day, I was feeling discouraged and I had reached out to a friend and asked her to pray for me. I asked her to just pray for me to feel joy in my life. Later that day, I went to a quarterly church meeting. We had dinner and they raffled off a few gift cards, gift baskets and other items. Before the announcer read out the numbers, she would say what was being raffled. There was a lot of noise in the room so I couldn't hear what it was. My number was called and when I got to the front of the room, I could not believe what I had won. It wasn't so much about the prize but the message and how attentive God is to prayers. Just

Why?

when you think maybe God is not listening, He sends you a sign in my case it was literally a sign that said "the joy of the Lord is my strength." (Nehemiah 8:10 NIV) What are the odds of something like that coincidentally happening? I had been reading that very Bible verse earlier that morning. And in that same way so many other times I have seen God show up.

When my grandmother died, I was devastated. I was consumed by an overwhelming, unfathomable sorrow. I felt like a part of me died with her. Right at that moment, He showed up and gave me peace and somehow, I was able to make it through that very difficult time. I can't explain it. It was just a calm and a comfort like no other. Only God can do that. When I am losing my mind, He gives me peace. When I'm afraid he frees me from fear, worry and anxiety. When I doubt myself, he gives me confidence, courage and boldness. When I feel abandoned, He comforts me. When everyone turns their back on me, He accepts me and goes overboard loving me. When I lost my job and was running out of money I made it through and he opened the door for me. When I found myself in a scary situation he protected me. When I screwed up things trying to do it on my own, he showed me mercy and got be back on my feet. He always gave

Chapter 10 – God

me what I needed so I could grow and change. When my friend walked away, he gave me new ones. He's the one that tells me to relax, that he's got me covered. He is the one that encourages me to laugh and not to be so serious. He is the one that tells be to live with boldness. He freely gives me all these things and so many others. When I am down, I just look at his promises and I get back up just one more time. That's what it's all about isn't it? To keep getting up and not letting anything tear you down. Being relentless is what moves you forward so you can make your impact in this world. Give God a shot He won't disappoint you. Don't let your circumstances get between you and God. Let your God get between you and your circumstances.

God is faithful

He is faithful to honor all that He promises. He is faithful to be who he says he is. He is faithful to forgive us no matter how many times we mess up. He is faithful to show us mercy. He is faithful to love us forever. He is faithful to call us into his family. He is faithful to protect us. He is faithful to stay by our side. He is faithful to make us winners. He is faithful to always be with us no matter what we feel, think or believe.

Why?

"God is not a man that He should lie" (Numbers 23:19 NIV)

Don't make anything your God

What is a god? It is anything that we obsess about. It is when you fill your life with things or people just to fill the emptiness that you feel in your heart. The most common gods of today are work, social media, relationships, money, pride and pleasing ourselves. Many of us also use these gods as a way to hide. We hide from our pain. We hide from our responsibilities. It is much easier to hide than to face the challenge of improving those parts of ourselves that need attention. Work, social media, relationships, money and pleasure seeking were never designed to be gods. If they are made gods, they make lousy ones because they are corruptible. These have a short shelf life. They cannot sustain you in the long run. They always disappoint.

The God of the universe should be your only God. Why do that? Because He is the only one that can fill the hole in your heart. The God that I have come to know; has always shown himself to be patient, loving and understanding. He accepts me for who I am. He has shown me true freedom; freedom from fear, from self-doubt. He has taught me to be a better person, a better friend, a better daughter and mother. He has been my friend when I've had everyone turn away. He has shown me the truth about myself and the truth about other people, good or bad. He has protected me even when I thought he wasn't even there. He has given me a purpose and a vision for my life. He has given me hope and joy. He has taken all the bad in my life and helped me to accept it and get past it. He has given me peace in the middle of turmoil. This is just but a little bit that he has done for me. And what he has done for me, he will do for you. It will be perfect and exactly what you need at the right time. And he will always answer your questions, maybe not how you imagined, but he will always answer.

Life Builders:

1. Say what He says, speak the promises in the Bible.
2. Think what He thinks, fill your thoughts with his thoughts.
3. Keep your eyes on Him at all times, don't lose your focus, don't get distracted.
4. Pray.
5. Keep believing no matter what.
6. Declare your victory.

Why?

7. Love Him.

8. Praise Him, this brings God's blessings to your life.

9. Trust Him.

10. Never give up, cave in or quit.

11. Stay joyful.

12. Stay grateful.

Life Killers:

1. Doubt.

2. Fear.

3. Anger.

4. Pride.

5. Complaining.

6. Criticism.

7. Legalism.

8. Self-pity.

9. Selfishness.

10. Negative thoughts about yourself.

Chapter 10 – God

God wants to shower you with his blessings. Every time you move into any of the life killers, I mentioned it's like putting up an umbrella that stops you from getting what God wants to give you.

Why?

Mom's Advice:	Look for God always, he is everywhere.
Key Point:	Trust in God with all your heart, look for him and he will guide you.
Guiding Principle:	"The instructions of the Lord are perfect, reviving the soul. The decrees of the Lord are trustworthy, making wise the simple. The commandments of the Lord are right, bringing joy to the heart. The commands of the Lord are clear, giving insight for living. "(Psalm 19:7-8 NLV)
Recommended Resources:	The Bible (AMP)

Notes: APPENDIX A

The Father's Love Letter

Adams, Barry. Fathersloveletter. 2024.
www.fathersloveletter.com Accessed 13 June 2024.

My Child,
  You may not know me, but I know everything about you. (Psalm 139:1 NLT)
  I know when you sit down and when you rise up. (Psalm 139:2 NLT)
  I am familiar with all your ways. (Psalm 139:3 NLT)
  Even the very hairs on your head are numbered. (Matthew 10:29-31 NLT)
  For you were made in my image. (Genesis 1:27 NLT)
  In me you live and move and have your being. (Acts 17:28 NLT)
  For you are my offspring. (Acts 17:28 NLT)
  I knew you even before you were conceived. (Jeremiah 1:4-5 NLT)

I chose you when I planned creation. (Ephesians 1:11-12 NLT)
You were not a mistake, for all your days are written in my book. (Psalm 139:15-16 NLT)

Why?

I determined the exact time of your birth and where you would live. (Acts 17:26 NLT)
You are fearfully and wonderfully made. (Psalm 139:14 NLT)
I knit you together in your mother's womb.
(Psalm 139:13 NLT)
And brought you forth on the day you were born.
(Psalm 71:6 NLT)
I have been misrepresented by those who don't know me.
(John 8:41-44 NLT)
I am not distant and angry, but am the complete expression of love. (1 John 4:16 NLT)
And it is my desire to lavish my love on you.
(1 John 3:1 NLT)
Simply because you are my child and I am your Father.
(1 John 3:1 NLT)
I offer you more than your earthly father ever could.
(Matthew 7:11 NLT)
For I am the perfect father. (Matthew 5:48 NLT)
Every good gift that you receive comes from my hand.
(James 1:17 NLT)
For I am your provider and I meet all your needs.
(Matthew 6:31-33 NLT)
My plan for your future has always been filled with hope.
(Jeremiah 29:11 NLT)
Because I love you with an everlasting love.
(Jeremiah 31:3 NLT)
My thoughts toward you are countless as the sand on the seashore. (Psalm 139:17-18 NLT)

Appendix A – The Father's Love Letter

And I rejoice over you with singing. (Zephaniah 3:17 NLT)
I will never stop doing good to you. (Jeremiah 32:40 NLT)
For you are my treasured possession. (Exodus 19:5 NLT)
I desire to establish you with all my heart and all my soul. (Jeremiah 32:41 NLT)
And I want to show you great and marvelous things. (Jeremiah 33:3 NLT)
If you seek me with all your heart, you will find me. (Deuteronomy 4:29 NLT)
Delight in me and I will give you the desires of your heart. (Psalm 37:4 NLT)
For it is I who gave you those desires. (Philippians 2:13 NLT)
I am able to do more for you than you could possibly imagine. (Ephesians 3:20 NLT)
For I am your greatest encourager. (2 Thessalonians 2:16-17 NLT)
I am also the Father who comforts you in all your troubles. (2 Corinthians 1:3-4 NLT)
When you are brokenhearted, I am close to you. (Psalm 34:18 NLT)
As a shepherd carries a lamb, I have carried you close to my heart. (Isaiah 40:11 NLT)
One day I will wipe away every tear from your eyes. (Revelation 21:3-4 NLT)
And I'll take away all the pain you have suffered on this earth. (Revelation 21:3-4 NLT)
I am your Father, and I love you even as I love my son, Jesus. (John 17:23 NLT)

Why?

For in Jesus, my love for you is revealed.
(John 17:26 NLT)
He is the exact representation of my being.
(Hebrews 1:3 NLT)
He came to demonstrate that I am for you, not against you.
(Romans 8:31 NLT)
And to tell you that I am not counting your sins.
(2 Corinthians 5:18-19 NLT)
Jesus died so that you and I could be reconciled.
(2 Corinthians 5:18-19 NLT)
His death was the ultimate expression of my love for you.
(1 John 4:10 NLT)
I gave up everything I loved that I might gain your love.
(Romans 8:31-32 NLT)
If you receive the gift of my son Jesus, you receive me.
(1 John 2:23 NLT)
And nothing will ever separate you from my love again.
(Romans 8:38-39 NLT)
Come home and I'll throw the biggest party heaven has ever seen. (Luke 15:7 NLT)
I have always been Father, and will always be Father.
(Ephesians 3:14-15 NLT)
My question is…Will you be my child? (John 1:12-13 NLT)
I am waiting for you. (Luke 15:11-32 NLT)

Love, Your Dad.

Almighty God

APPENDIX B

God's Prayer for You

John 17:20-26 Amplified Bible (AMP)

[20] "I do not pray for these alone [it is not for their sake only that I make this request], but also for [all] those who [will ever] believe and trust in Me through their message, [21] that they all may be one; just as You, Father, are in Me and I in You, that they also may be one in Us, so that the world may believe [without any doubt] that You sent Me.

[22] I have given to them the glory and honor which You have given Me, that they may be one, just as We are one; [23] I in them and You in Me, that they may be perfected and completed into one, so that the world may know [without any doubt] that You sent Me, and [that You] have loved them, just as You have loved Me. [24] Father, I desire that they also, whom You have given to Me [as Your gift to Me], may be with Me where I am, so that they may see My glory which You have given Me, because You loved

Why?

Me before the foundation of the world.

²⁵ "O just and righteous Father, although the world has not known You and has never acknowledged You [and the revelation of Your mercy], yet I have always known You; and these [believers] know [without any doubt] that You sent Me; ²⁶ and I have made Your name known to them, and will continue to make it known, so that the love with which You have loved Me may be in them [overwhelming their heart], and I [may be] in them."

APPENDIX C

Get to know GOD

Here are some verses that speak of the attributes of God.

God Answers (Isaiah 58:9)	God Keeps (Deuteronomy 7:9)
God Bestows (Proverbs 8:21)	God Knows (Matthew 6:8)
God Blesses (Deuteronomy 14:29)	God Leads (Isaiah 42:16)
God Blots (Isaiah 43:25)	God Lifts (Psalm 146:8)
God calls (1 Thessalonians 4:7)	God Listens (Psalm 10:17)
God cares (Nahum 1:7)	God Loves (Psalm 37:8)
God Cleanses (Jeremiah 33:8)	God Opens (Deuteronomy 28:12)
God Clothes (Isaiah 61:10)	God Pours (Isaiah 44:3)
God Comforts (Isaiah 51:12)	God Preserves (Psalm 41:2)
God Corrects (Job 5:17)	God Protects (Psalm 41:2)
God Counsels (Psalm 32:8)	God Provides (Psalm 111:5)
God Covers (Psalm 91: 4-6)	God Purifies (1 John 1:9)
God Delights (Zephaniah 3:17)	God Rejoices (Isaiah 62:5)
God Delivers (Psalm 37:40)	God Remembers (Psalm 111:5)
God Disciplines (Proverbs 3:12)	God Rescues (Psalm 91:14)
God Encourages (Psalm 10:17)	God Restores (Psalm 71:20)

Why?

God Fills (Job 8:21)	God Rewards (Proverbs 19:17)
God Forgives (1John 1:9)	God Satisfies (Psalm 132:15)
God Gathers (Deuteronomy 30:4)	God Saves (Isaiah 49:25)
God Gives (Matthew 11:28)	God Speaks (Isaiah 30:21)
God Guards (Psalm 97:10)	God Strengthens (Isaiah 40:29)
God Guides (Psalm 73:24)	God Sustains (Psalm 55:22)
God Heals (Hosea 14:4)	God Teaches (Isaiah 54:13)
God Hears (Psalm 69:33)	God Upholds (Psalm 37:24)
God Helps (Psalm 37:40)	God Watches (Genesis 28:15)
God Holds (Psalm 73:23)	God Works (Romans 8:28)
God Increases (Deuteronomy 7:13)	

APPENDIX D

How to pray when you don't know how

Pray the word of God. There is power in the word. It is like a nuclear cloud. It goes out and its power changes everything. Praise God first for who He is and for everything He has done even when it still hasn't happened. Pray believing that what God has promised will happen because God is faithful, loving and truthful. Read the Bible so you will know what God promises you in every area of your life. Pray for healing, prosperity, favor, protection, for whatever you need.

Use the prayer in John 17 (The high priestly prayer) as a guide (see Appendix B). It is the prayer that Jesus prayed before he went home to be with His heavenly father. You can also use The Lord's Prayer as a guide. (Matthew 6:9-13 AMPC) And if you need some help, use some books to help you learn how to pray effectively. My go to book has been, *The Weapons of Our*

Why?

Warfare by Kenneth Scott. This book has been a literal life line for me over many years. Another gem that I found for prayer is Stormie Omartian's the *Power of a Praying Woman*. These are great resources to help you pray. One good way to pray is to pray for our leaders, in government, church, school, work, and at home. Pray for your family and children. Finally pray for yourself and your requests.

APPENDIX E

How to find a safe church

Simply put Integrity. Does the church do what church is supposed to do? Does it love others? Does it show compassion to all? Does it take the hurting and love them? Does it reach out to the community? Does it feed the hungry and clothe the poor? Does it make a difference in their own community? Does it teach the truth of God's word?

There are many people who don't set foot in a church because they had a bad experience in the past. Someone who was supposed to be nice instead hurt them, embarrassed them, shamed them, or made them feel small. No one should ever be treated that way. My heart breaks when I hear these stories. Unfortunately, all too many of us have been let down. Everywhere you go whether it's church, work, or otherwise the fact is that there are different types of people. There are the fakers; these folks are in church but real church is not in them. This type of person is characterized by being superficial. What they say and do don't match. There are the self-involved; they are so caught up in their own lives that they do not show love in their relationships. These folks can be well intentioned but hurt others because they can seem uncaring. The other group of people are unaware; they are believers and have faith but they don't demonstrate the qualities that characterize a follower of Christ. Finally, those that are the real deal; even though they are in the process of growth with God. Love, humility, truth and grace are present and increasing. That person is the kind that brings healing in other people's lives. Please remember that churches are made up of people. People are imperfect. Don't expect a perfect church; there is no such thing. You need to know who you are dealing with and set the appropriate boundaries. There will always be people in your inner circle and those in your outer circle. Be wise about who you put where. And even then, expect surprises because there will be some. You might be thinking why even bother? We all need to feel connected. We are all here to share our gifts. What is uniquely yours is placed in your care for the good of others. Don't deny yourself or them the opportunity to benefit from giving and receiving.

Appendix E – How to find a safe church

When you are ready to look for a church. Here is a great list of things to look for from Dr. Henry Cloud and Dr. John Townsend.

1. Grace is preached not condemnation.

2. Truth is preached without compromise. No sugar coating it.

3. Church leaders are aware of their own weaknesses. They are open about their hurts, pains, failings and humanity. They don't act like they have it together. They are not closed to change or confrontation.

4. The church uses small groups to touch people's lives and focus on community.

5. The culture is of forgiven sinners not of self-righteous religious people.

6. The church is not self-contained it is networked to the community and other professionals.

7. The teaching is relational. Relationship with others is seen as part of spirituality as well as a relationship to God.

8. The teaching sees brokenness, struggle and inability as normal part of the sanctification process.

9. There are opportunities to serve others through a variety of ministries.

Cloud, Henry & Townsend, John. *"Where are the safe people."* Safe People, Zondervan, 1995, p.165.

Why?

Finally, pray for guidance from the Holy Spirit. Ask God to lead you to the place where you will thrive and make a difference. Thriving and making a difference are really important when choosing a family of believers.

About the Author

GRISELLE PAZ is an Emmy-nominated writer and producer. She stands as a light in the realms of broadcast writing, literature, and personal development, seamlessly blending her talents to leave an indelible mark on the world. She has contributed her creative prowess to major broadcast organizations, including ABC, CNN, and, Univision, earning recognition for her exceptional work as a writer and producer. Griselle's written works extend beyond the screen; she has also graced the pages of several literary magazines. Her journey through the media landscape reflects a commitment to excellence and a passion for storytelling that goes beyond the ordinary.

As a certified life coach, Griselle channels her passion for personal and professional transformation empowering individuals to rewrite their own narratives.

You can find out more at:

https://speakoutsolutions.net/

or for more about the author visit: https://lifelightpress.com/authors

www.ingramcontent.com/pod-product-compliance
Lightning Source LLC
Chambersburg PA
CBHW060504090426
42735CB00011B/2109